LOVE AND POWER

Also by Bud Harris, PhD

Sacred Selfishness: A Guide to Living a Life of Substance

Aging Strong: The Extraordinary Gift of a Longer Life

The Journey into Wholeness: A Jungian Guide to Discovering the Meaning of Your Life's Path

Becoming Whole: A Jungian Guide to Individuation

Reflections from the Chrysalis: A Collection of Essays for the Path to a Well-Lived Life

The Midnight Hour: A Jungian Perspective on America's Current Pivotal Moment

Facing the Apocalypse: A Call for Outrageous Courage, Love, and Compassion

Confronting Evil: A Jungian Guide to Searching for Light in the Heart of Darkness

Radical Hope and the Healing Power of Illness: A Jungian Guide to Exploring the Body, Mind, Spirit Connection to Healing

The Search for Self and the Search for God: Three Jungian Lectures and Seminars to Guide the Way

Cracking Open: A Memoir of Struggling, Passages, and Transformation

The Father Quest: Rediscovering an Elemental Force

Resurrecting the Unicorn: Masculinity in the 21st Century

The Fire and the Rose: The Wedding of Spirituality and Sexuality

Students under Siege: The Real Reasons Behind America's Ongoing Mass Shootings and How to Stop Them

Coauthored with Massimilla Harris, PhD

Into the Heart of the Feminine: Facing the Death Mother Archetype to Reclaim Love, Strength, and Vitality

Like Gold Through Fire: Understanding the Transforming Power of Suffering

The Art of Love: The Craft of Relationships: A Practical Guide for Creating the Loving Relationships We Want

LOVE AND POWER

A Guide for Cultivating the Values of the Heart

BUD HARRIS, PHD

DAPHNE PUBLICATIONS • ASHEVILLE, NORTH CAROLINA

DAPHNE PUBLICATIONS, AN IMPRINT OF SPES, INC.

Harris, Clifton T. Bud
Love and power: a guide for cultivating the values of the heart / Bud Harris

ISBN 979-8-218-22361-8 Non-fiction
1. Jungian Psychology 2. Self-Help 3. Body, Mind, Spirit

Spes, Inc, Asheville, NC

Cover design by Courtney Tiberio
Interior layout by Susan Yost

Author's Note:

You are kindly invited to read this book. These are diffi-cult lessons in love and power I have learned personally and through over half a century of professional educa-tion and practice that I want to share with you. As chal-lenging as these lessons have been for me to develop and live, they have become the foundation of a life that is more rewarding than I could have ever imagined. Again and again I've learned that our lives are restored and redeemed when we learn to let our hearts speak.

Writing, I have found, provides me a way to focus and understand my life experiences, and also better compre-hend what is happening to me and around me. This book is my effort to bring a new theme out of my thinking and feelings. While most of its content has been previously ex-plored in my newsletters or other books, here I am bring-ing those concepts about love and power together to chal-lenge our understanding of society, ourselves, and how we need to grow into a new future. I am very concerned about the darkness that is being revealed and acted out in our society that has gone unrecognized for too long. As we as a nation have turned away from love, we have entered a wasteland of the spirit so intense I am afraid we may never find our way home again. But I don't want us to forget that in our country's history, even in the face of darkness, we have been able to find our better angels and create a future that has often inspired humanity.

I hope my writing will challenge you profoundly and help you clarify the meaning of love and power, both within and toward the personal challenges and chaotic times we are living in. Above all I continue to hope it

helps you create a new vision of the future and a new
hope that draws you to commit to it.

Bud Harris, PhD
Asheville, North Carolina

Contents

Foreword

The first time I heard the term **love warrior** I experienced a real awakening. The phrase resonated with me immediately. As I understand it, a love warrior is a person who is committed to love as a central value in life. Love is indeed a complicated concept on many levels, such as the love of life, of oneself, of each other, of the divine, and much more. To be a warrior is to use your power, to develop skills, focus, strength, purpose and the determination to serve a higher value. To become a love warrior, then, we must know who we are, be grounded in self-respect and respect for others, in self-acceptance and the acceptance of others. Learning this transforms us, and helps us grow beyond our false beliefs, passivity, wounds, and narratives that limit us, grounding us in a way that brings confidence, clarity, and a total commitment to our visions and values. Becoming a love warrior challenges the very depth of who we are and who we want to be, so we can stand for our highest values against the destructive forces threatening life, without becoming such a destructive force ourselves.

Through decades of intense experiences supported by education, professional training, and practice,
I have learned that without the early love we need
in our lives—to nourish our feelings of safety, trust
in our surroundings, and have confidence in ourselves—we will have trouble having a real sense of
who we are. As a result, all too often we will end
up seeing ourselves through the eyes of others in
order to feel real without realizing how vulnerable
this makes us.

Strength of character is based on a foundation of
positive traits that are morally valued and contribute to the fulfillment of ourselves and others. The
foundation for developing character is love. Without the foundation of love that leads to character
that leads to knowing who we are, we are left running scared, developing a false self, defined by outside influences. We are also left in the grip of a past
we cannot escape and will not openly admit. Without character, we try to avoid our personal, and in
the larger sense our collective dark challenges by
repressing and denying them. We seek to avoid the
creative visions and the discomfort and suffering required to make needed changes and reformations.

In Jung's terms, we thereby create a lot of neurotic or sickly suffering in our efforts to avoid
the transformative pain of facing our reality, our
wounds, healing and the birth of a new way of living. This process is as true for our society as it is for

us personally, and in both cases impoverishes our spirit. Reclaiming our foundation of love and becoming love warriors opens the vistas of a new horizon of hope and fulfillment for all of us. It brings light into the darkness.

This book is written for those, like me, who know that the best meanings of love and power have been lost in our culture for a long time. It is written for those who are seeking to rekindle the flame in our hearts and find a better foundation for living. It provides a rapid overview for one of the most important quests in our lives.

The first lesson I offer is dedicated to facing our reality. Marketing, media, religious and political propaganda have been very good at creating our weaknesses and making us think that what we have and how we appear can define and fulfill us. At the same time, they help drown out the voices of our inner reality and the needs of our hearts. But, as we will see, facing our true reality and how the lens we see the world through filters our view of reality may surprise you. To fully appreciate the forces that shaped the lens through which we think we are seeing our reality may require a long apprenticeship in self-examination. But the reward is to lift our lives beyond the ordinary and to open our eyes to a new perspective upon ourselves and the world.

"Where love stops power begins, and violence and terror." These words from Dr. Jung (*Collected*

Works, CW, vol. 10, para. 580) have puzzled and troubled me for over five decades. I see them everywhere as I work, observe people and society. I see them in relationships: in marriages, people and partners, parents and children, brothers and sisters, in business, between different groups of people and throughout political factions. These words of Dr. Jung echo loudly in my soul in the middle of the night. They shock me out of my sleep, and I fear the influence that violence and terror and the battles for power are taking in our culture. But I don't surrender easily. These fears remind me I must not let love stop. We must remember that we are born to be loved and to love. And, as parents to our children, ourselves, our society and the planet, we are born and challenged to nurture love. Even when it may seem impossible, we must remember we have this healing power within us. Our great religious traditions, each in its own way, have told us this truth for centuries. I have learned through many decades of personal and professional experience that hope can be found. We can learn to accept, understand and live love as the foundation of human destiny.

Many years ago, I reached an important turning point in my journey when I came to the realization there are two stories that make up my life. The first story is the one I commonly tell myself and other people about who I am. The second story seemed to develop by itself, even though it came out of my experience.

The first story I worked hard to develop as I grew into adulthood and found a place in the grown-up world. The second story is the one Dr. Jung discusses in his autobiography, *Memories, Dreams, Reflections* (p. 117). This story is often hidden from our everyday awareness; thus, Dr. Jung calls it a "secret story," one that he considers to be like a 'rock' that often blocks or 'shatters' our lives. This buried and frequently denied story is about our deeper inner experiences of pain, loss, love, expectations, loneliness, and terror. It may also be about the resilience, the potential, or the heroism within ourselves than we fear to recognize. Make no mistake about it. Every life has such a hidden story.

Stories I have heard from people whose addictions drove them into treatments such as Alcoholics Anonymous or whose suffering or desire for a greater experience of life pushed them into Jungian analysis seem like tales of heroes and heroines to me. These people have the courage to accept the grace of that warrior life-force which tries to drive us through blocks, stagnation, and disasters into a greater experience of life and continual evolution. Jungian analysis is a quest for life, for becoming, for evolving through conscious engagement with our inner and outer experiences. It is a quest to use our whole being to discover the truth of our lives. This journey must be taken because we have been hiding the truth about our reality and our experiences from ourselves. So, the truth of our reality must be discovered before it can be faced. In Jungian psychology we call this process "confronting our shadow." Confronting our shadow increasingly helps us see reality more clearly and reveals how our former world view was shaped by our secret story.

The influence of the dominant attitudes of our society and the unseen stories they create also shade the way we see the world. All too often we have adopted these influences and stories as part of our personality without realizing it. For example, in general, our society isn't programmed to encourage reflection. Time spent focusing on our inner lives, growth and wholeness, or searching for self-knowledge, is not respected. At best it is only tolerated as a method for problem solving or symptom relief. Society prefers to rush on, stay busy, and focus on acquisitions, material and financial status, or even entertaining experiences. Overall, these attitudes cause us to focus more on our public faces than our inner reality. This forward and outer thrust in our society comes together to make it hard for too many of us to see the secret stories of suffering we are collectively creating…stories that are currently blocking and fracturing the character of our society.

Confronting our shadows is vitally important because it is the path to fostering truth and reconciliation within ourselves and our society. This task is not an easy one because it must also bring our two stories together as the foundation for who we are and who we may become. Through the lessons in this book, we will examine this process closely. We will learn how to look at the inner story that, up to now, we have hidden, generally out of fear. Perhaps that fear is of confronting the pain and loneliness we have carried for a long time, or perhaps it is the fear of facing the real potentials we have ignored or denied. In either case, the journey will be one into wholeness, which means living into the capacities we have for being fully engaged in the blood, sweat, tears, and joys of life and loving every minute of it.

The secret story that Dr. Jung talks about is usually about intense experiences like love, terror, and power. He explains that when we lose the aptitude for love it is replaced by a sickly need for power. He noted that the fire of wounds caused by *lack of love* in our early lives sleeps in the dead ashes of our hearts and then rekindles in the darker areas of our lives if it has no other place to go. If we can't awaken to *the need for* love as the basic story in our lives, *that need* will find other outlets in sickly quests for power. Our fire may appear in disguise as emotional symptoms of distress or as excesses such as fundamentalism, addictions, compulsive sexuality, overly busy lives, relentless ambitions, and even hate. These destructive potentials that can erode our existence give an important warning about how crucial it is to understand what true self-love must be in the foundation of our personal and collective lives. The fundamental reality that I will explain is **that we are born to love and be loved,** and that starts at the minute we come into the world. Our parents may have been better or worse or have totally failed at loving us, but the truth is we have all failed to see this fundamental reality for a long, long time. But now we have more knowledge about who we are and it is crucially important to our lives, health, and the future of our children and grandchildren that we accept this—we are born to love and be loved.

We must also take responsibility for what we know and take action to implement it. To begin with, the action we must take is not to attempt to change the world, but to change ourselves. The fundamental journey of change is within ourselves. It is to work through our shadows, our challenges, our willful naiveté, our willful ignorance and to learn what it means to love ourselves as the foundation for loving others and life. Dr. Jung expresses clearly that all great changes must begin with each individual, because society and its attitudes are a summation of those of the people who make it up. When enough of us make the effort to become self-aware, confront and integrate our shadows, and become grounded in self-love, the changes our society needs will begin to happen without crusades, or our crusades will have the foundation to support real changes for the better.

Becoming a Jungian analyst was my way of dealing with the confusion, conflict, and anguish in my own secret story. Facing my secret story began the process that led to fulfilling what was waiting to be awakened in me, to see what I needed to do and what I needed to become. The first thing I needed to do was to step onto the path to develop my potential for truly loving myself. This short book and its lessons are meant to help you begin one of the most fascinating aspects of the journey of life.

I have learned that trying, no matter how hard, to love life and put on loving behaviors like a clean shirt or a new public face, not only never works but frequently turns out to be destructive. In addition, learning how to integrate my rage and despair has become the power that energizes my creativity and leads to a creative and loving life. Both love and creativity require the courage to expand and often break through the boundaries and the rigid framework of old values and attitudes buried in our secret stories that our rage and despair are trying to challenge. Cultivating a devotion to being a love warrior is like water flowing into a pond. When the pond is full the water will overflow and begin to venture out into the world.

I have never lived nor imagined living in a time when our country was gripped by such a great contagion of insecurity, confusion, and fear. Never could I have imagined so many people being alienated, angry, even to the point of being enraged, and so bitterly opposed to fellow citizens. I am old enough to know some of our history, to remember that we called my parent's generation, though it was far from perfect, "the greatest generation." They knew in simple terms that what makes America great is its intentions for good. I know that each one of us make up America, and, thus, for our country's intentions to be good, enough of us must have good intentions. The true foundation of good intentions is the power of love. This knowledge reminds us of what we can become if we strive for it.

My efforts in this book are to share with you what I have learned about developing the love and power within ourselves. Releasing the power of love can heal us personally and collectively and become the foundation for a creative future. My hope is that this book will guide you in journeying to the source of love and strength within you. Thank you for joining me.

Renewing the Promise of Life

I can remember a night in 1960 like it was yesterday. About eleven-thirty my wife nudged me awake and told me it was time to go. Our week had been busy because it was the last week of my final quarter at Georgia Tech. We were also in the ninth month of her pregnancy. At the time, we were living in-town in Atlanta in a garage apartment in the lovely Virginia-Highland area. As soon as we were up, we phoned our obstetrician's service and found out he was already at Crawford Long Hospital with another delivery and would be expecting us. I was soon in the car with the motor running and on the verge of a panic attack. Meanwhile, my wife was calmly collecting the things she had prepared to take with her to the hospital.

We arrived at Crawford Long in about ten minutes and quickly went through the admission process. As was the usual procedure in those days, she was taken into the maternity ward and I was told to take a seat in a somewhat bare waiting room with old magazines and a couple of lonely-looking men. I wouldn't see my wife again until it was all over. The doctor did come out and greet me cordially and then disappeared. He was a quiet, gentle, confident-appearing man, well into middle age. I waited for a couple of hours, essentially in a trance. Then the doctor reappeared, assured me my wife was fine, congratulated me and said we had a fine baby boy. Then he invited me to come in and see the baby. As I did, there was a nurse behind a glass partition who picked up this tiny red form of life for me to see. I was filled with awe and terror. This same feeling of awe and terror returned when each of my two daughters were born.

I understood the feeling of awe. Seeing the arrival of new life into the world naturally inspired that feeling in me and still does. But even though I realized that being a father would be full of challenges and responsibilities I didn't understand the deep, almost instinctual feelings of terror. It took me several decades of intense self-integration in my personal journey to realize that each of those tiny sparks of new life was born to be loved and to love.

The beginning of new human life is meant to be the beginning of a story that is a love story. This beginning is meant to be the foundation for that love story. Deep inside of me, maybe in my heart, even in my bones, I was terrified because I knew that I didn't even know how to live that story for myself and therefore for my children. Having children and encountering life's challenges and traumas caused me to have to stop and question all of the values and assumptions I had structured my life on within a decade of that night in 1960.

Within a few more years I turned to the spirit of C. G. Jung's individuation process as the beginning of a new path for structuring my life. Since that time, I have had a growing devotion to the spirit of life supported by this process as being one of challenge, learning from suffering, growth, and love. The underlying principle of Jungian psychology is that our life story, if it is truly lived, brings about the realization of our inner and often unconscious potentials. Unfortunately, love as a life-supporting value has become repressed into the unconscious life of our social character. From the Jungian perspective we see that one of life's greater goals is to seek the wholeness that is potential within us by bringing into consciousness what we have repressed or dimly know about ourselves.

More often than not these potentials are characteristics that are undeveloped or underdeveloped in our lives, and they need nurturing to help them grow. In every lesson that follows I will explain that process more fully and guide you into it. On that night in 1960, I didn't realize it, but my capacity to love was dimly known and underdeveloped even though I considered myself a loving person. In actuality the journey of individuation included discovering and developing my capacities for love as a fundamental part of discovering and following the inherent, unique pattern for development that lies within me. This process, as you can imagine, results in the unfolding of our personhood in both our inner and outer worlds.

A fulfilling life is one that is continually bringing our inner potentials into conscious expression and completion. Understanding and experiencing loving and being loved are the bedrock for the foundation of a fulfilling life. There are few traditional textbooks, scientific systems, or religious techniques that can do any more than give us a little help along the way as we seek the kind of self-knowledge that leads to individuation. The knowledge required for this task can only come through increased conscious awareness based on our experiences in living and our relationship to our interior life. Each lesson in the book is devoted to cultivating this process.

Self-understanding and self-realization are key concepts in the Jungian approach to living, but they are not simply intellectual terms. They must be supported with courage and strength and married to the values of the heart. Originally, they emanated from the "heart of the physician" in Dr. Jung, who felt great compassion for people's suffering and, as himself a wounded healer, he wanted to help them and us find healing and wholeness, so as to be at home in ourselves and life. As Jung grew into his later years, it is clear that his heart expanded into the future of humanity and culture. I share these profound concerns. In this spirit of concern, I am writing this book which reflects my journey of discovering, understanding, and developing the places of love and power in my life and the society in which I live.

– BUD HARRIS, PhD

Jungian Ideas on Love and Power

Generally, we tend to think of love and hate as opposites. But in reality, they are often closely connected because they both contain intense emotional involvements. For example, I might say I had a love-hate relationship with my father. This combination could then mean we had a passionate relationship that shaped and formed both of our lives. From another standpoint, some people consider indifference as the opposite of love. Indifference signifies a coldness to life that often shows how we are walled off within ourselves. But one of Jung's most significant insights is that the true opposite of love is **power**. "When love rules there is no will to power; and where power predominates, there love is lacking. One is the shadow of the other." (C. G. Jung, *Collected Works*, vol. 7 para. 78)

Jung went on to explain that on many levels we understand life and our experiences in terms of opposites—such as black and white, male and female, strong and weak, and so on. Thus we can see love and power as opposite ends of a dynamic emotional and energetic continuum.

LOVEPOWER

Using this continuum, Jung shows that the more one-sided we become in this pair of opposites, the more neurotic we become in respect to the direction we are moving in. The more neurotic we become, the more intense our symptoms of distress become. In the case of moving toward the pole of power, as our social character has been doing for decades, the more our diminished capacity for love will manifest itself. The more our social character is oriented toward power the more the symptoms of wounded love or the devaluing of human beings will show up as symptoms of alienation, a general state of fear, anger, rage, and violence in our citizens. These symptoms are the signs of a societal disease. This reality means that while we must try to alleviate the symptoms we must also try to understand and heal the root causes of the disease. Otherwise, our efforts to control the symptoms can actually increase the disease.

For example, when our social character moves too far toward power more and more people begin losing heart, faith in our institutions is diminished, and more people feel devalued. They feel that they don't matter to our social institutions, and that their safety, security, community, and future opportunities are slipping away. In fact, this is exactly what has happened in our society for decades as the increasing symptoms of rage, fear, aggression, and political destructiveness are showing us.

The real answer for us is that we must find the courage to examine ourselves and see how each of us form this social character. We must confront our collective value system and change the direction that is currently focusing on power and its components of material success and achievement. In other words, we must transform the heart of our society. Since we individuals made up our society, we must begin with ourselves, and this book maps that journey as I have learned it.

Love must be united with power to be strong. We must passionately stand for, defend, and bring the values of love into our lives and to form a society that holds every life sacred. Uniting love and power is a profound joining of two of our greatest instinctual energies in their positive forms. I picture the yin-yang symbol of two interacting positive forces within a circle, a container of wholeness, as being appropriate for this unification of love and power.

Once combined in this manner, these energies become passionate and lead us through the darkest experiences and directly into transformation, creativity, and new life. The path for this unification for each of us is the theme of my writing. Our power instinct gives us the strength of purpose to become love warriors and helps each one of us realize our most important human potential to love and be loved—our birthright.

Lesson One

Facing the Truth of Our Reality

This is the first of nine lessons I want to share with those of you who feel like the meaning of love has been lost in our culture for a long time. I have put them together, if I am honest with myself, to remind me that the quest for love in its greatest sense needs to be the central theme in my life. These lessons are also written for you, if you, like me, are seeking to rekindle the flame in your heart and find a better foundation for living. I believe that together they will provide a rapid but challenging overview of the most important quests in our lives and encourage our hope for the future.

The reality that I have had to face with anger and deep sadness is the black hole in the heart of our society. It cannot be filled with achievement or problem solving because the seriousness and number of problems is simply overwhelming. It can only be filled with love coming from a change of heart in our society. It can only be filled by remembering the heart of our founding principles: that all of us were created equal, endowed by God with the inalienable rights of life, liberty, and the pursuit of happiness; and our government's sole purpose is to secure these rights. Our founding principles gave us a vision of a future to be fulfilled that challenges each generation to carry its promises forward. We individuals make up our society as a whole, so this challenge, this change of heart needed today, is one we must all face.

I grew up in the era of the Cold War. During those years, deep inside of ourselves we were scared of nuclear annihilation all of the time. Many people built bomb shelters, and children had practice alarms of "duck and cover" in school. But to be truthful, I am more scared today than I was then. My fear today is because so many people are in angry and aggressive denial of the reality we are living in and the destructive future we are heading toward. Even worse is my feeling that we have turned away from our humanity and love as our most important virtues.

In my lifetime I have seen us regress from a people who could come together—not perfectly, but effectively—to stand up to any challenge no matter how difficult or daunting, to a society that is almost the opposite: fragmented, angry, self-centered, and callous. During the pandemic's onslaught hundreds of thousands of our families, friends, and neighbors suffered and died simply as a result of our failure to come together and confront our reality effectively. So, through the lens of my Jungian perspective I began to search to understand my fear and our collective regression from what was once considered America's greatest strength.

Time after time in his writings Jung emphasized that the truth of our reality must be faced before we can begin the process of healing, transformation, and change. We find little evidence of that truth being looked for in our world today. As a result, our society is now on a suicidal journey. Our circumstances and suffering are begging us to face the truth of our collective reality. It is vitally important for us to seek to understand it and how to respond to it with resolve. I have also learned from my own struggles and professional experience that we must seek out and confront the components of our collective, societal shadow and understand how, all too often without realizing it, we are participating in forming and supporting it.

Without being aware of it we have also created a culture that is eliminating the great feminine principle of Eros (love), which supports life and our potentials of healing and transformation. As a natural consequence of this murder, we are killing our humanity. Once we accept the truth of our reality the next questions are—how can we stop doing this, and what can we do to reverse our course?

Jung explains what happens when we allow power to begin replacing love (CW, vol. 70, para. 480), "Where love stops power begins, and violence and terror." When we try to face our reality, it is helpful to remember that Jung also taught that the more we become identified or possessed by one characteristic such as power in our personality, then human nature will begin to provide a corrective compensation. While we are focusing on daily living and paying less attention to what is really happening beneath the surface in our personal and collective lives the more forceful the compensatory message becomes. In this case, when love stops, the symptoms of the imbalance, violence, terror and things going wrong increase. These are symptoms that show us that serious changes of heart, mind, and action are needed to reverse the course and bring us true healing.

From this brief explanation I think it becomes clear that as the conflicting quests for power in our society continues love disappears and if we do not reverse that course, we are inviting chaos, terror, rage, and destruction. *Making a reverse course* is not easy. It takes a lot of courage to face the ingrained values in our society and in ourselves of the pursuit of power, individualism, materialism, and achievement at any cost. To let ourselves be transformed into new, more-human beings takes courage as well. William Butler Yeats wrote, "It takes more courage to examine the dark corners of your own soul than it does for the soldier to fight on the battlefield." It takes even more courage to examine the dark corners of our collective soul. We need **love warriors** to face and reverse the course we are on.

Jung used the word Eros to describe the archetypal feminine principle. Eros means having a keen interest in relationships and a prevailing attitude that works for conciliation and reconciliation. It supports healthy interdependence on every level of life. Eros evokes self-integration, subjectivity, and concern for individuals. Eros is rooted in the material universe and the earthy feminine qualities of love, receptivity, and transformation, i.e., new life being born. Eros supports the love of life, individuals, and the pains of bringing forth the future. Eros and love do not lead us to an end of the challenges of human life but they support us in facing them, living through them and when feasible being transformed by them in ways that enhance our growth, character and wisdom.

The needs for love that permeate our lives, the needs of the feminine heart, must awaken the spirit of true masculine strength that is meant to stand for life, to nurture and protect it in all of us, men and women. I know very well this kind of strength is not just some ideal to pursue; its development is true self-responsibility. Through long life and almost half a century of professional experience I have learned that love and strength are the only real pathways to feel at home in ourselves and secure in life.

For example, we, as a society, seem to have forgotten that we learn about love in childhood. Our home atmosphere is our school for learning how to love and be loved. For several generations, in the anxiety and pressure of the ways our lives have been evolving, we have lost touch with how to honor and love our children in a way that will help them become strong adults, secure in their identities, and capable of loving and being loved. If we haven't grown up in an atmosphere of love we will not know how to love and teach love to our children, no matter how well we may care for them. We will not know how to appreciate ourselves by finding the experience of parenting loving and fulfilling.

✦ ✦ ✦ ✦

Over the years I have realized that as much as failures may brutalize my self-esteem, my greatest transformations began with failure. I have also learned to overcome some of my fear of encountering these events. Sometimes I even desire them. Through these experiences, I have learned that we are defined by what troubles us, not what reassures us. I recognized long ago that I have never been transformed or learned anything significant from success. So I generally look at failure as the first step on a new journey. This is a journey we need to begin now. Moreover, as I have emphasized, we need to face these moments of change head on, with courage supported by a love of life and energized by an inner quest for self-awareness and growing consciousness.

Self-awareness and growing consciousness are crucial because, no matter what we think, we all live in a self-inflicted condition of limited awareness of reality. Hindu philosophy calls this condition *maya*, or a state of illusion. For us to be truly aware of our reality, we have to know a great deal about our shadows and the dominant psychological complexes that shape our worldview. Let us look at an explanation that, although greatly oversimplified, describes how this state of illusion can come about.

If we don't get the love, safety, and affirmation we need in the first eighteen months of life, we will internalize the feeling that the world is a hostile place and we won't be capable of feeling secure in it (severe traumas while growing up may have a similar effect). These experiences generally become a dominant complex. This complex governs how we see the world and puts us into an adversarial relationship with it. We may find ourselves facing conflicts with a fight, freeze, or flight response. We will have an irrational distrust of other people and institutions. We will often be vulnerable to social, political, and religious manipulations that play on our fears. When we feel weak or diminished, we may find that explosions of anger give us a sense of power and standing in the world. We are afraid of feeling vulnerable or weak and of not having our right to exist validated. Anger becomes our protective shield.

If we don't become aware of our dominant complexes, we will always be susceptible to outside manipulation on many levels. Good advice is often to "face reality and deal with it." But if we haven't recognized and worked through our dominant complexes, what we think is reality is usually far from it. This brief explanation illustrates that self-awareness and facing the truth of our lives are crucial for living a meaningful and fulfilling life. The very same is true for our social character and the advancement of our culture.

To become aware of our personal complexes and shadows—while difficult and often shocking—helps us realize potentials we haven't known, and that transformation always means a change of heart. We will be faced with the task of creating a new structure of psychological and spiritual values that define who we are and how we are going to live. New meaning must be found for our lives, and this whole challenging and often painful process must become a meaningful experience in its own right.

In my profession we know a lot about the foundation for loving and being loved. But in our society in general we seem to ignore the fact that knowledge should give us the power to change our lives for the better and bring us new joy and satisfaction in raising our children. Knowledge has the power to help us see how important it is to give ourselves the time and space to love and to accept the challenges of cultivating our humanity.

Our first challenge is to wake up and face the truth of our reality before it is too late! We are being challenged to develop what I like to call outrageous courage, love, and compassion. I believe they are outrageous because in our society today they are counter-cultural. Courage, love, and ambition are attributes of "character." Having ambition and drive are different from having character, as is being resentful, angry, and defiant or being indifferent to what is really happening around us. We are challenged in the words of James Baldwin to "begin again" and honor and live the great feminine principle.

We are challenged to become **love warriors** and it will be our ongoing quest in the next three lessons. Great love warriors have dared to challenge conventions and their own value structures, and have pursued things that seemed impossible. I have loved the term "love warrior" since the first time I heard it from Dr. Cornel West, a love warrior himself. This transformation is not impossible if we begin to take a passionate look at ourselves and the circumstances around us. For example, before seeking political success Franklin Roosevelt gave half of his fortune to create a hospital for children with polio in Warm Springs, Georgia. Martin Luther King, Jr. turned city streets into sacred spaces that transformed history. Also, Mother Teresa, in a different way, brought love and healing to the least of the people in her society. Maya Angelou turned a broken life into a strong love song for all of us. These are a few examples of love warriors. The potential to become love warriors is possible for all of us. It lies deep in our hearts waiting for us to have the courage to find it. It may be helpful if you take a few minutes to think of the names of other love warriors that have inspired us. Please feel free to include people that may not be well known but touched your life. I hope this series will help each of us become a love warrior within our own heart and the world we live in.

Thoughts and Questions to Ponder

- What were your thoughts and feelings when you read: "there is a black hole in the heart of our society"?

- Please take your time and explore what it means to you and for our future when I write: "we have also created a culture that is eliminating the great feminine principle of Eros, love, the source of life…"

• Facing reality and accepting it are generally thought of as the first steps toward healing, growth, problem solving, and creating positive change. All of these require an accurate understanding of reality. Too often, though, we are unaware that understanding reality is no simple task. What do you think of the statement, "Self-awareness and growing consciousness are crucial because no matter what we think, we all live in a self-inflicted condition of limited awareness of reality"?

• How has the discussion about the influence our early experiences have on our worldview and our response to events expanded your understanding of our perception of reality?

• Does it make sense to you that for us to accurately understand reality, we first have to develop an accurate understanding of ourselves and the forces that have shaped and directed us? My books Sacred Selfishness and Becoming Whole are devoted to this task.

• How does the following statement affect you: "If we don't become aware of our dominant complexes, we will always be susceptible to outside manipulation on many levels"?

Other Thoughts?

Lesson Two

Love's Foundation

Somewhere in our not-too-distant past, we as a society began to lose our capacity to love. I believe we began losing it in the very place and atmosphere where it is meant to begin. There is no other closeness in human life like the closeness of the mother and baby. We see it clearly reflected in its best sense in the images of the Madonna and child. This image of the mother and child is the archetypal image of the bond where love is meant to begin. Physically and spiritually mother and baby are only a heartbeat away from each other. When the mother's heart is serene the baby's heart is untroubled. And they are joined in the powerful nature of the bonding hormone oxytocin through skin-to-skin contact. Within this bond we are meant to learn two things—that we are lovable and how to begin loving. When the mother's heart beats in stress or fear or is otherwise troubled, the baby's heart picks up her restlessness or fear. When her heart is serene the baby feels safe and comfortable. These heartbeats, or the absence of them, become the foundation of who we are and our struggle to become our future selves.

But what happens when our mothers don't or aren't able to fully respond to our needs? How does it affect us that in our society the feminine principle, or love in general, is so wounded that being what we call in psychology a "good enough" mother—not perfect but confident and secure—is almost impossible. This early wound is a basic wound to the very nature of who we are, personally and collectively. What can it mean that we now have generations of mothers and fathers who may have been well cared for materially but never experienced the true nature of the early love they needed to feel safe and valued. Deep fears, self-doubts, self-criticism, desire for hidden control, power drives, and depression are sure to follow early shortages of love. The destructive power of this wound is amplified because it initially comes from the very person whose positive image and influence is fundamentally and vitally important to us at the beginning of our lives. This person is the one we were born to expect to love us and whose love lays the foundation for our capacity to love, to feel secure in life, and to trust its experiences.

We all know that life is complex and the mother-infant relationship can be disturbed for any number of reasons, such as early deaths, illness, separations, or deprivations due to many kinds of crises. This compels me to point out the importance of fathers in this picture. Fathers, familial and cultural—what should be the real patriarchy—play a crucial role in fostering this important human relationship, the foundation of love in the lives of our children. In older times the cultural fathers took responsibility for their roles. The positive side of the patriarchy should uphold life and security, protect women and children, and encourage health, education, the development of character and art. Today's patriarchy is a negative, destructive force that has lost its heart and integrity. As love warriors, men must fight to regain the heart and spirit of true fatherhood.

As love warriors, we all need to learn how to protect our families from fear. In a society where our identity, and therefore our self-worth, is based on achievements and accomplishments, anxiety—which is fear—accompanies us daily. All too often this is a fear of being shamed as we feel we are failing to live up to expectations that will help us feel approved and valued. Our culture's wounding and belittling of the feminine and its values has led many mothers to mistrust the world and men to a greater extent than ever before. This mistrust inevitably becomes part of the emotional fear heritage of our children. To make things even worse, our media amplifies terrible events to the extent that fear permeates the atmosphere we live in every day. Within the last fifty years we have created a society with an economic system that essentially requires both parents to work, almost guaranteeing stress for younger families and an overly demanding burden on single parents. In the long run, as human beings, our primary sense of security through life comes from love, caring, trust, and emotional closeness. But our sense of family, our original school of love, is seriously threatened more than ever.

Society didn't take the importance of love as a foundation for life into consideration when I had my children decades ago. The experts in that era thought that babies were to be controlled and shaped. They were to be trained to eat and be nurtured on schedules. We were advised not to pick them up every time they cried because they were supposed to learn to fit into the regimen of their parents' work and busy lives. Of course, this approach didn't work well in my experience and our attempts left us tense, frustrated, and feeling like failures as parents. Training babies in such a way actually indoctrinated them on a very primal level into believing they can't trust that their needs will be met, they can't trust their own ability to get what they need, and they learn not to trust love and life. The image of the Madonna and child teaches us something else. It is so profoundly moving because it represents the archetypal image in all of us that shows that new life and the mother need to live in a space of safety, love and security. But it rarely seems to occur to us that this love, safety, and security must be created by us.

I know that it is easy for me to say as an analyst that as a society we are too individualistic, competitive, power driven, achievement-oriented, and materialistic. While all of these things are true there is another side to these statements. It is the side of personally living in this landscape. I've lived in this society, worked in it in many areas, and raised a family in it. I know what it feels like to have jobs become more insecure, to have retirement prospects become uncertain, healthcare costs to be a hovering threat, hope for your children's futures to be shaken, college costs to seem beyond your fingertips, and more. Plus, I am not even poor. I know what it is like to be indifferent to larger issues because you already feel overwhelmed, are facing too many demands, and are working your life away. Indifference in this case is a symptom of facing too much, trying as hard as you can and having political knowledge slip through the cracks. We are burning ourselves up and out and that is another reason we, as love warriors, need to transform the heart of our society and our lives before the growing collective rage in our midst damages our culture beyond repair.

Yes, our children are living in fear and our inner unity and security are split, even fragmented in many cases. Almost all of us are over-involved in the demands of our outer lives at the expense of our inner lives. Without realizing it the demands of our daily lives, as we see them, have caused us to become so alienated from our own natures that we have practically forgotten they exist. Or we may be caught in a cycle of frustration because we realize we are split from our authentic selves but cannot figure out how to cultivate and nourish our relationship with ourselves. These problems started in the beginnings of our lives. Mother and child as symbol, metaphor, or in concrete reality are simply no longer safe in our world.

The road to understanding myself and getting a true perspective on reality has required a difficult deprogramming of my indoctrination into thinking that I should have a positive attitude, appear happy, not burden others with my feelings, and be able to control and direct my life. It has taken courage to face these necessary changes in myself, and so does the humbling effort to continue to confront the wounds to love within me. It took courage to face the very discomforting fact that I have been wrong or negligent about a number of things rather than face the complex demands of being an active, responsible adult and citizen. Over the years I have betrayed some of my deepest feelings, values, and potentials. It is also humbling that after eight decades of living I need to start over again to learn who I really am. If we can learn how to re-imagine ourselves based on the deeper truths of who we are, we will have a better foundation for re-imagining many areas in our personal and collective lives. In this way, we will be able to bring continuous renewal and vitality into our lives and culture.

As I think about my history, the reality we raise our children in, and the knowledge that we as a society ignore, the words written by the modern brain researchers Thomas Lewis, Fari Amini, and Richard Lannon in their book on attachment theory and brain research, *A General Theory of Love*, come to mind: "From birth to death, love is not just the focus of human experience but also the life force of the mind, determining our moods, stabilizing our body rhythms, and changing the structures of our brains...love makes us who we are and who we can become."

To become a love warrior, we must first learn to face, heal, and love ourselves where love has been wounded in us. If we do not do this first, we will find it hard to imagine that love really has the power to change things. That is why I write so carefully about cultivating self-love in Lesson Six. If we fail to heal ourselves and rebuild the foundation of our self-love and trust, fear will always lurk deep inside us and fuel our anger and compulsions for power and control. To become a love warrior, we must learn that the presence of pain in our lives isn't a sign of failure or a reason for shame. It is a call for healing and growth, to use our best human powers for mindful reflection and change.

Love does heal and it must begin within ourselves. To face the wounds to love within ourselves takes courage to even admit they exist. We must become wounded healers in the culture we live in, with the knowledge of what has caused our wounds and how to heal them. Our inner experience is the foundation we need to know that love really has the power to change everything. On this road as love warriors, we soon learn that choosing self-examination and growth is embracing the love that heals.

Thoughts and Questions to Ponder

- Have you, like many of us, taken love for granted during your life and thought that it should come naturally?

- What thoughts and feelings come to mind for you when you read my opening statement? "Somewhere in our not-too-distant past, we as a society began to lose our capacity to love."

- Have you ever considered what it may mean to never experience the kind of early love we need to feel safe and valued?

- Write in your journal what you think about this statement: "In older times the cultural fathers took responsibility for their roles. The positive side of the patriarchy should uphold life and security, protect women and children, and encourage health, education, the development of character and art."

• Write in your journal what comes to mind when you read my closing statement in this lesson: "On the road as love warriors, we soon learn that choosing self-examination and growth is embracing love that heals."

Other Thoughts?

$$\overline{\text{Lesson Three}}$$

Power Supporting Love

Iam afraid that the white, educated middle and upper-middle class now seems to have lost its spiritual ground of caring about the welfare of others. Pursuing the idols of achievement, materialism, money, and security seems to be its new religion. Putting a premium on serving the community, lifting others, and finding joy in trying to educate and empower every citizen seems to have gone underground. As caring for each other by those who have the real power to influence our communities has become secondary to self-interest, the energy of those people who are becoming side-lined and alienated is erupting through emotionally and physically violent outbursts, suicides, and addictions.

We live in a time when my social group, which could affect so much change in our society, has generally misunderstood and become uncomfortable with the use of power. The wounds to love from the ways the values of our society are structured have limited and hurt our most important instinctual foundation. This foundation is made up of three instinctual patterns. The first is the mother instinct, which must be cultivated from and through our primal relation to our mother and will then internally support our ability to like, nourish, and take care of ourselves throughout our lives. The second is the father instinct, which is our instinctual need to become self-reliant, autonomous, and independent. The third is the power instinct, which when developed in a healthy manner gives us the ability to experience ourselves as having value because we are able to succeed and achieve certain desired goals. Through this process we gain a sense of confidence in living our lives.

It may surprise you to realize that power is essential for all living things. The word power comes from the Latin "posse," which means "to be able." When our power instinct begins to awaken and grow in the fertile field of a family's love it is crucial in molding our feelings of self-worth. It gives us the ability to experience ourselves as having value because we increasingly feel we are able to pursue desired goals and achieve them. By that process we feel we are able to gain a measure of control over our lives and future. As we mature it is our power instinct that can give us the sense of security that comes from a feeling of being able to be and do on our own, independent from our parents and later institutions that may substitute for them.

Let us look at how our power instinct is wounded in the school of love we call families; several things can happen. To begin with, as this instinct becomes wounded it turns on us in its negative form. Then it can paralyze us with self-criticism and perfectionism. It can drive us to become passive and withdrawn from life. It can cause us to become controlling and always trying to force a happy outcome, especially by being a pleaser. It can leave us fearful of conflicts and without the necessary potential for aggression to defend our self-esteem and stand for what we think is right. Our wounded power instinct can also drive us into a pursuit of achievement, seeking self-assurance and security in a manner that is doomed to never be enough. Ultimately, however, as I discovered, it can cause us to pause, begin to look inward, and give us the confidence to risk the inner journey.

Coming from the social group I grew up in, my pursuit of healing my sense of power and the ability to be fierce in defending the values of life helped me learn how to value my instinctual nature and my body. The increasingly positive power to pursue my goals and to feel at home in life and with myself opened the door to my personal authenticity, learning to be kind when kindness is warranted and aggressive when it is required. When necessary, such personal power becomes fierceness. Being fierce was not something that I was brought up to be comfortable with. It wasn't "nice," especially in relationships. Yet as I have learned it, it has increased my confidence in myself, clarified my vision in murky times, and made it easier to love myself and life. Most of all this kind of inner strength can give us a spirit that opens our hearts and prepares us to love. As our power is developed in a positive way it supports the growth of compassion that awakens us to the healing power of service, to our spiritual needs, and to the needs of others. Love that grows from a firm foundation, whether from our families or from our healing journeys into self-love, cultivates the knowledge within us that love in its greater sense is about service—love in action—which enlarges us and contributes to life.

In the 1960s I believe we saw power and fierceness used in what we considered as morally wrong and destructive ways. Examples were Vietnam, riots, burning cities, police brutality, assassinations, and poverty. In one shock after another at these events my social class tried to become anti-fierceness. Many of us, especially mothers, didn't let their kids play with guns or play war games and so on. Many parents didn't want their sons to play football and risk getting hurt. Unfortunately, blindness can come to us far too easily. Trying to avoid the pain of needed confrontations, seeking easy answers that appear obvious, and being reluctant to strongly question ourselves never serves us in the long run.

Without realizing it we began to repress the positive development of the power instinct in our children. This instinct is needed to build their ability to become self-disciplined, to take risks, to overcome fear, to endure pain and make sacrifices to achieve worthwhile goals, and to thereby become self-responsible adults. We made a fundamental error in judgment. We failed to realize that destructive power is the reaction of someone or some groups that feel powerless. Powerlessness means we feel insignificant to other people and therefore of little value to ourselves. In our adolescents and young adults and in many older people there is a widespread loss of confidence in our power to make a difference in the world surrounding us emotionally and politically. Admitting this reality to ourselves is very painful and we often try to avoid it in many angry and destructive ways.

We arrived at this place collectively by looking at the symptoms of misused power and not at the root causes of it. We have never examined the collective fear that drove us into the Vietnam war, the injustices behind the riots, the deep shadow of hate in our society behind the assassinations, nor have we looked at the past traumatic stress we experienced collectively. In facing our challenges from violence, we need to become love warriors determined to seek out the true cause of our society's rage and violence and to solve or heal these problems at their root levels, as we both contain and learn from the destructive uses of power.

While I am writing about our power instinct, I remember how fairy tales and legends, our age-old stories, show us the conflicts of power and the ordeals of becoming fully human. They can offer us many lessons, evolved over time to help us on our way. The legends of King Arthur have been favorites of mine since boyhood. I remember when King Arthur was standing with Merlin on the ramparts of Camelot in T. H. White's *The Once and Future King*, a lovely book written for the eternal child in everyone. As they were discussing the future, the young King Arthur had a startling insight—that might must be used for right and not might makes right. "Might for right" became the motto for him and his knights. In the story, as Arthur began his kingship, he had to bring many conflicting parts of his kingdom under control and into harmony around the symbol of unity, the round table. To become a knight, one had to prove himself as competent in power and in strength, show skill at arms, and exhibit the ability to bear hardship and pain. Prospective knights also had to adopt the code of chivalry, a system of courtesy and respect for others, especially for women. They were dedicated to defending against injustice and defending the poor and disadvantaged, along with women and children.

Before going into battle, they were often "shriven," meaning going into the Christian ritual of confession, usually with a monk in the forest. When they used their power, they wanted to be assured they weren't being driven by negative or evil forces. Every year they met on Pentecost (the Christian day celebrating the day the Holy Spirit came to humankind) to renew their fellowship and vows of service to causes beyond their personal interests. Finally, to save king and country from being a wasteland, they undertook the quest for the Holy Grail in order to bring the symbols of power and spiritual passion together to renew the life of the kingdom. In our quest to become love warriors we can learn a lot from this venerable legend.

As love warriors we must also bring power and the passion of love together to transform our hearts, the heart of our society, and renew the best values of our humanity. Think about how different our world can become if we really have the support of love warriors.

Thoughts and Questions to Ponder

- How seriously have you thought about the place of power and fierceness in your life? Have you, like many of us, thought of power and fierceness as primarily negative instincts? How do you see it now?

- Can you write a short history of your power instinct, how it was born, what effected its growth, how you would like to experience it today?

- What are some of your reflections on the story of King Arthur and the value structure entwined in it? Can you see it as an archetypal story, as important for women as it is for men?

- Write in your journal what comes to mind when you think about this: "As love warriors we must also bring power and the passion of love together to transform our hearts and the heart of our society, and to renew the best values of our humanity."

Other Thoughts?

Love Chooses Life

The essential quest of a love warrior is to never settle for an interior wasteland caused by a discouraged or barren heart. We must be dedicated to seeking the Holy Grail, the life source, in the forests of our interior lives. Choosing life means becoming fully engaged in living with body, mind, and heart. For us to be fully engaged with life we must be fully committed to our inner lives and resources. This means we must be on the journey to discover and mature our capacities for passion and compassion, for love and strength. Becoming a love warrior is to confront our fears, our suffering, our despair, and the shadow sides of our lives, our culture, and our history. And it is to do this with the confidence that comes from the good we have done and are still capable of doing.

To be a love warrior is to see every problem and failure and the accompanying suffering, as Jung affirmed, as bringing an opportunity, a challenge, and the possibility of becoming fully human. They present us with the possibility of widening our consciousness along with the necessity of saying goodbye to our childish, naive trust in the habits of our past. If, as we become love warriors, we see the new problems life forces on us as questions meant to deepen our understanding of life's meaning, they will increasingly provide us with opportunities to separate from the false security of our conventional past. It has been true that we often preferred quick fixes to long patient work. But the gift of consciousness, self-awareness, and a more profound awareness of the society we live in will give us the vocabulary and the resources to understand what our ancestors did not. This knowledge should compel us to own and address what is wrong today.

To be a love warrior is to seek to confront our shadows. In Jungian terms, facing our reality means we must face our shadow, the things we have repressed, denied, and hidden. We must face the darkness we are and have been, the wounds to our spirit, hearts and souls, personally and collectively. In pursuing this quest, we must also remember that this process is seeking awareness, not condemnation; let us not forget the best of who we are and have been, and that our shadows also contain the repressed potential for the best we can become.

Speaking of love is often like pressing a finger on the bruises we have collected in our lives. A love warrior learns that a deep love of life doesn't come to us easily. It grows slowly as we learn to truly understand ourselves, our torrents of emotions, the forces that shaped who we are, the darker, destructive sides of our personalities, our denied positive potentials, the knowledge that life is a process, and that love and respect must go hand in hand. Self-knowledge brings us the power to live in an authentic, fulfilling way. It brings the capacity to deal honestly, thoughtfully, and lovingly with other people. Self-knowledge brings to the surface the essence of what life is. It enables us to recognize the emotional games we play with each other, to confront reality, and to have compassion that is born out of the knowledge of our own torments. Without self-knowledge our notions of love often reflect needy psychological pursuits, idealistic fantasies, or sentimental hopes. Without self-knowledge we cannot truly choose either to be fully alive or to truly love. Growing self-love and self-knowledge are like water flowing into a pond. When the pond is full, the water will overflow and begin to nourish the world.

Love warriors come to understand the essential meanings of aggression. We see this clearly in the 1960s when the assassinations of our visionary and moral leaders stole our future from us. And the school shootings began. These tragedies compelled two of our greatest psychologist thinkers and social commentators, Erich Fromm, PhD (*The Anatomy of Human Destructiveness*) and Rollo May, PhD (*Power and Innocence: A Search for the Sources of Violence*) to study and explain what was taking place in our society to produce these staggering catastrophes. The crucial question for a love warrior is: "What is taking place in our society to produce such murderous, destructive rage and despair?"

Now, let us take a closer look at what this statement means. Dr. Fromm, writing on human destructiveness, classified aggression into two categories, benign aggression and malignant aggression. Malignant aggression is destructive and attempts to control life by destroying life and the spirit of life. It is power oriented and is generally the result of a sense of helplessness and impotence that causes a person to attempt to transcend the negative states of neglect, rage, and alienation through violence. Such violence compensates for the feelings of impotence and alienation.

Malignant aggression is usually paranoid, hoards material possessions and seeks to build up power and destructiveness. In extreme cases such people seek escape from being trapped by doing violence to others, to institutions, and even to themselves. The parallels on a national level are obvious, especially as people in groups act and vote against their self-interest. As malignant aggression penetrates our society, anxiety generates a greed for power that subtly replaces eros. This greed negates life by always demanding more.

Robert Kennedy, a love warrior who was stolen from our future by hate and violence, asked us to pray during the night after Dr. Martin Luther King, Jr. was gunned down. In closing his brief, heartfelt address he said:

> What we need in the United States is not division; what we need in the United States is not hatred; what we need in the United States is not violence or lawlessness; but love and wisdom, and compassion toward one another, and a feeling of justice toward those who still suffer within our country, whether they be white or they be black.
>
> So I shall ask you tonight to return home, to say a prayer for the family of Martin Luther King, that's true, but more importantly to say a prayer for our own country, which all of us love—a prayer for understanding and that compassion of which I spoke.
>
> We can do well in this country. We will have difficult times; we've had difficult times in the past; we will have difficult times in the future. It is not the end of violence; it is not the end of lawlessness; it is

not the end of disorder...

Let us dedicate ourselves to what the Greeks wrote so many years ago: to tame the savageness of man and make gentle the life of this world.

Let us dedicate ourselves to that, and say a prayer for our country and for our people.

It is very important for us to reflect on and absorb the words in this prayer. Dedicating ourselves to this cause introduces us to the meaning of benign aggression. Benign aggression means using power, strength, skill, and determination in defense of life, to preserve life and to have a spirit of adventure in the support of life. Love warriors understand the imperative of life is to grow, heal, and renew. As human beings this imperative means we must ally ourselves with life, love, and the courage to face the struggles growth and renewal entail. What happens if we are not open to this imperative to grow? If we fail to grow and renew, we will stagnate and begin to deteriorate, no matter how good or successful we seem to appear. The assassins in the 1960s robbed us of the models of great love warriors who were showing us how to create life in a broader form. These love warriors transformed the meaning of courage from raw aggression and conquering to preserving the sacredness and dignity of life, pursuing moral and spiritual journeys, and justice, love in action. The courage to stand for life, not for conquering or ruling, is also the courage to explore ourselves and our culture deeply and then to act with self-awareness. We are challenged in the tradition of King Arthur to use "might for right" to pick up the swords of our strength and discrimination and use them to choose, protect, and defend love as the foundation for life.

Now we have arrived at this very important point. The question always comes up: "What can I do?" In the commencement address at Queens College in 1965 Senator Robert Kennedy said to the graduates, and through the years to us today:

> We must remember our revolutionary heritage. We must dare to remember what President Kennedy said we could not dare to forget—that we are the heirs of a revolution that lit the imagination of all those who seek a better life for themselves and their children; that we must seize the chance to lead this continuing revolution, not block its path; that we must stand, not for the status quo, but for progress.
>
> The essence of the American Revolution—the principle on which this country was founded—is that direct participation

in political activity is what makes a free society.

Freedom, for the founders, was not merely negative, the absence of arbitrary restraints. Freedom for them was active and positive—the power of each individual to take part in the government of the town, the state, the nation—as Jefferson said, "not merely at an election one day in the year, but every day," every man was to be "a participator in the government of affairs."

At this point, I want to invite us to face these considerations. In today's crisis we must ground ourselves as love warriors in our inner journey and at the same time seek out other people struggling with these problems at home, at church or temple, in community centers, or by seeking to bring people together in conversation. We must look for the cracks in the walls with patience and compassion for people who want us to do better in the crucial areas we are facing. Big things usually start small and they will grow if we can, in diversity, begin to discuss the tough questions causing our alienation, fear, and quests for power and violence. These discussions can grow into hope if we each do what we are able to do—have the courage to speak up, speak to the best in us to defeat those who speak to the worst in us; organize, vote, and call our leaders to account—there will be more of us tomorrow and next month and we'll be getting closer to the potentials in our hearts.

Now as I finish this lesson, I am aware that we need so many things. We need compassion and reconciliation. We need a warrior spirit to return love to its proper value in our humanity. But the first thing we need is to be sure we have a firm foundation for becoming a love warrior.

In the next five lessons we will build our inner foundation in courage, self-love, compassion, and in healing alienation. I invite you to join me in waking up and committing with all our hearts to transforming the heart of our society.

Thoughts and Questions to Ponder

- Please think some more about this quotation and write a few responses to it in your journal: "Becoming a love warrior is to confront our fears, our suffering, our despair, and the shadow sides of our lives, our culture, and our history. And it is to do this with the confidence that comes from the good we have done and are capable of doing."

- What kinds of thoughts and feelings come up in you during the discussion of malignant and benign aggression? You may want to write a few of these in your journal. Do you understand the essential meanings of aggression?

- Please take some time to consider your thoughts about each line in Robert Kennedy's prayer.

- How seriously have you thought about the challenge in the final quote from Robert Kennedy to remember we have a revolutionary heritage of direct participation in political activity, which is what makes a free society?

Other Thoughts?

Lesson Five

Cultivating Courage

In my various writings I have described my father as a storm-driven man. Coming from a common background, he boldly stepped into the challenging struggles of life, education, marriage, the Great Depression, a world war—a life of trials. He was driven by courage and desperation. Our relationship was passionate and conflictual. But I miss him. His spirit, passion, desperation, and courage flow through my veins.

I have spent a lot of time during my life thinking about passion, desperation, and courage. It is clear to me why, many centuries ago, Aristotle asserted that courage is the most important virtue: without it we can't practice any of the others. Courage is the nearest star, casting the light that energizes our growth. The great poet, educator, and humanitarian Maya Angelou says that we must be courageous about facing our personal histories, that we must find the courage to care and to create internally as well as externally. And, as she says, we need courage "to create ourselves daily as Christians, as Jews, as Muslims, as thinking, caring, laughing, loving human beings."

As an analyst, I have been concerned for decades by our society's dwindling courage, its polarization of aggression, and its disregard for the daily choice of good over evil. We seem to have lost sight of the lofty expanse of our founding documents. Instead, the focus has narrowed to a shallow version of the "pursuit of happiness," and the rationale for our behavior has become pragmatic, problem solving, and conflict oriented. In politics, business, and our personal lives, many of us have become "players" or "onlookers" rather than having the courage to be full participants. As a result, our sense of right and wrong seems to be fading away, and we are losing the ability to act with courage and resolve toward the major problems and threats in our own front yard.

Courage in its fullest sense becomes a **foundation** when we open ourselves to experiencing life and ourselves in their wholeness. Love, loyalty, living creatively, living our authentic values, caring for ourselves and others all require taking risks, and such risks call for courage of the heart. The word *courage* comes from the French word *coeur*, which means "heart." It is courage that pumps the life force throughout our being. Below are seven principles that are necessary to help us understand the more profound meanings of courage and that can guide our development of it every day.

1. **Have the courage to honor fear.** Fear is an important part of our nature. Fear is a dragon we have to face again and again in a life that we are living wholeheartedly. Just as we find other strong feelings, or even illnesses, are the seeds for our growth, the same is true for fear. It takes outrageous courage to accept the fear within ourselves. We must learn not to repress it, deny it, or look for the easiest way out. It speaks to something important within or outside of us, and that leads us to my second principle. But, before reading on, you might take some time to answer this question: As you were growing up, how were you taught to deal with fear, and how do you deal with it now?

2. **Have the courage to understand fear.** If we fail to understand our fears and their origins, they will become a mounting force in our unconscious that will constantly undermine our self-confidence, our abilities to face needed changes and growth, and our ability to appreciate ourselves and the opportunities to enjoy life. Seeking to understand fear doesn't mean

to embrace or give in to it. Fear is seductive, and if we allow it to unconsciously drive us, we can become seduced by the false gods of achievement, money, security, appearances, magical others, and magical leaders. Keep in mind that understanding fear is a spiritual journey because it is so easy to quickly sell ourselves out in the face of fear. Journaling about your efforts to understand the force of fear in yourself and in our society is an effective and rewarding way to challenge the worldview you actually live by.

3. **Have the courage to let yourself live with fear.** The truth is that life is difficult. If we choose to be fully alive, we must have the courage to take risks and encounter unforeseen challenges. This is reality, even though we seek the illusion that a well-planned, carefully lived, good life will be trouble-free. But neither God nor Buddha nor any other great spiritual leader or tradition guarantees or even encourages a trouble-free life. In fact, attempting to keep that illusion can contribute to the arrival of an apocalypse. Throughout history our great spiritual figures inspire us to grow through our painful experiences by seeking to understand their lessons. Although we may think it is safer to avoid trouble than

to seek it, trouble often ends up finding us anyway. Remember, courage means acting, loving, and being compassionate even when we are afraid. Without fear, courage cannot exist.

4. **We need courage to create.** Whether we are creating art, a new business, or a new life, we need rage and passion to break out of the chrysalis of fear, pride, conventional thinking, our need for approval, our misguided value structure, or whatever is holding us back. Creativity requires the courage to concentrate all of our passion, our love, our anger, our rage, and our hatred combined with our sensitivity and our thoughtfulness.

   When rage and hate are destructively acted out, they may be wasted, they may be a defensive outlet, and they may be creativity gone wrong. Or they may be an apocalyptic symbol. You might ask yourself if you have a bias toward rage that keeps you from realizing its positive and symbolic value.

5. **Have the courage to listen to your shadow.** Our shadows are those parts of ourselves that we have repressed, denied, and rejected into our unconscious. They are, or we fear they would be, socially unacceptable,

shameful, threatening, embarrassing; we have put some of our potentials in these categories because we are afraid that if we tried to accept them, they would take us out of our comfort and safety zones. We might see them as symbolized by enemies, beggars, thieves, prisoners, rich people, tyrants, strangers, and so on in our dreams. In fact, in real life it is the disenfranchised people, the alienated people who can tell us the truth about what is wrong in our society. The same is true in our inner society, and we must have the courage to get to know these parts of ourselves so we can understand the unconscious structure that governs our lives. This is a very important point to think about. Both personally and as a society, we tend to prefer willful ignorance over finding the outrageous courage to face the painful realities we are creating. To face the truth about our shadows and reconcile with them personally and as a society is the path to a new structure of values, meaning, and purpose. The path begins with courage.

6. **We need courage to honor the individuation instinct.** To choose life is to choose individuation. For Jung, our most basic instinct is the instinct for developing consciousness, the in-

stinct for individuation—in other words, the instinctual life force calls for the complete development of our full potential. Honoring that instinct requires outrageous courage because it entails a lifelong process of psycho-spiritual life, death, and rebirth. Individuation confronts us with conflicts, life events, and situations that call for us to challenge ourselves, to see reality in new ways, and to recreate ourselves and our worldview. It takes courage to choose life and give up safety and comfort as signs of spiritual and material success. I accept it as a challenge that still comes as a shock but is reality in its most rewarding sense.

7. **We need courage to love and be vulnerable.** Love demands courage because it always makes us open to pain and loss. A love of life opens us to the sufferings of life. But denying or trying to avoid and escape such suffering has two other consequences. First, according to Jung, the effort to ward off true suffering is what creates neurotic suffering. Second, if we close the door on suffering, we close the door on real joy. For many years in our society, the pursuit of a kind of driven happiness has been the theme. As a result, we are a society with very little knowledge of joy. To love in

a substantial way requires courage because it leads us to the full experience of being human. It takes outrageous courage to love the light within ourselves, the potential to love.

✦ ✦ ✦ ✦

The troubled time we are living through is the death of an age. It is up to us to midwife the birth of a new age, and if we fail at this task, we will see the destructive aspects of the difficulties we are facing increase dramatically. Shall we, as we feel our foundations quaking, retreat into fear, despair, or indifference? Or shall we try to cover our deepest fears with angry outbursts and tribal wars? If we do, we will have abandoned our duties to ourselves, to those we love and care about, to humanity, and to the future. If we do, we will have turned our backs on the teachings of our greatest religions. If we do, we will have forsaken the American ideals of freedom, equality, and liberty. If we do, we will have relinquished *hope*, which is grounded in a person's and a community's ability to work for something because it is good.

Or shall we seize the courage necessary to renew our personal and collective values of the heart—sensitivity, caring for one another, awareness, and responsibility—in the face of radical challenges? Shall we, through strengthening ourselves, building our awareness, and broadening our understanding, participate in forming a new social character for our country?

We are called upon in the midst of these times to destroy the old conventional approaches and to create new selves and a new society and to right many old wrongs we have experienced personally and collectively. We are being called and pushed into new territories where there are no well-worn paths; no one has been there before and returned to guide us. To commit to "a whole new approach to life" is to live into the future by stepping into the unknown, and because there is no road map to reassure us, this requires outrageous courage.

Courage opens doors to hope, to an orientation of the spirit, to the imagination, to love in all of its complexities, and it sees beyond the horizon.

Thoughts and Questions to Ponder

- How seriously have you thought about courage during your life? Have you generally, like most of us, thought it was simply being brave in dangerous situations? Have you, like most of us, thought it means not having fear?

- What does this statement bring to your mind? "Courage in its fullest sense becomes a foundation when we open ourselves to experiencing life and ourselves in their wholeness. Love, loyalty, living creatively, caring for ourselves and others all require taking risks, and such risks call for courage of the heart." Does it stir your feelings?

- Were you surprised when you read these statements? "Have the courage to honor fear." "Have the courage to understand fear." "Have the courage to let yourself live with fear."

- How did you respond when you read the following: "We need courage to create. Whether we are creating art, a new business, or a new life, we need rage and passion to break out of the chrysalis of fear, pride, conventional thinking, our need for approval, our misguided value structure, or whatever is holding us back"? What are some ways you have built up rigid structures that now limit your vigorous and creative response to the readings, to aspects of the apocalypse we are experiencing, or to your own life situations? Are these structures affecting your responses right now?

- It might be helpful for you to journal a personal response to each one of the seven principles in this section on courage and the ones coming up on love and compassion.

- As you reflect on this section about cultivating outrageous courage, what do you feel about commitment to a whole new life?

Other Thoughts?

Lesson Six

The Healing Power of Self-Love

In the Foreword of this book I noted two quotations from Jung that have confronted me for decades. The first one is, "Where love stops, power begins, and violence, and terror." The second one is that "the individual's feeling of weakness, indeed of non-existence, was thus compensated by the eruption of hitherto unknown desires for power." These statements are ever present in the back of my mind as I reflect on the apocalypse we are in.

Not long ago I re-read *The Fire Next Time* by James Baldwin. It had been years since I first read it. On page 22 actually, I was jolted by these sentences: "White people in this country will have quite enough to do in learning how to accept and love themselves and each other, and when they have achieved this—which will not be tomorrow and may very well be never—the Negro problem will no longer exist, for it will no longer be needed."

I was stunned. This is one of the most profound

passages I have ever read. In a few sentences he shifts the ground of our racial problems and the responsibility of White people into a challenge I had never thought of. But its truth is beyond dispute. He also challenges African Americans to love themselves in a similar way.

Two thousand years ago a revolutionary called Jesus gave us a great commandment, the second part of which is to "love your neighbor as yourself." We have paid a heavy price throughout history for not learning what this simple-sounding but incredibly profound commandment means if we seek to live by it.

When I was young, I thought self-love was the most natural thing in the world. But it is not. With maturity, I learned better. Self-interest and self-denial may seem natural, but they are more likely driven by our complexes and wounded hearts. Self-love is another story. Self-love is one of the most difficult things in the world to achieve. This commandment, in a simply straightforward way, challenges us to a series of quests that are demanding. Yet it promises more than we can easily imagine. Jung, as I quoted him earlier, explains where failure in these quests leads us. Baldwin outlines the promise of these quests when self-love becomes the foundation for mediating our relationships.

I remember very well when the idea that Jesus's commandment directs people to love themselves in order to love their neighbor became very popular and widely discussed. This encounter with what it might mean to love myself was in the early 1970s. When it came right down to it, I realized I didn't have a very good idea of how to love myself. At the time I was just starting graduate school, and we were studying the works of the great humanistic psychologist Dr. Carl Rogers. Rogers taught that the ingredients for a healing and growth-sustaining therapeutic relationship were to be genuinely engaged in the relationship, to be emotionally congruent in it, to be emotionally warm in it, to be empathetic and understanding in it, and to give the other person "unconditional positive regard." Well, I concluded, if I don't really know what it means to love myself, it won't hurt to try to have a good therapeutic relationship with myself since I'm studying how to do this with other people anyway. So, I began reviewing these steps nightly in my journal and practicing them on myself. I particularly like the idea of giving myself unconditional positive regard. I had always thought the idea of unconditional love was infantilizing, and I wanted my self-love to be strengthening. This practice had a profound effect on me and, I believe, on my development as a therapist all those decades ago.

Self-love, in its fullest sense, becomes a burning necessity when we open ourselves to our wholeness. It becomes the foundation not only of our love of life but also of the family of humanity and its future. I want to share with you seven principles that I have used in my lectures and books that are necessary to open the door to self-love one day at a time.

1. **Remember, love is difficult,** the poet Rainer Maria Rilke explains, in contrast to the sentimental way we like to think about it. Review your thoughts about love. Do you think it should just bring happiness and ease, or at least security? Do explosions, struggles, and failures make you think love has failed? Life isn't easy and love can't be easy either.

2. **Cultivating self-love is an odyssey with moments of difficulty and joy.** It's an excursion into knowing ourselves, into asking whether what we are doing is adding to or diminishing our feelings of self-worth.

3. **Self-love challenges the boundaries that we have fenced ourselves into, such as practicality, conventional wisdom, and other people's perspectives.** We must gently ask ourselves whose voice we are really hearing in our head. Is it the voice of our heart or something bigger, like our true Self?

4. **Self-love isn't self-indulgent.** It isn't shopping sprees, outlandish vacations, sneaking sweets,

or pouting moods. It is the commitment to growing in self-knowledge and in our capacity to love. Remember, taking the time for reflection isn't egocentric. It is the key to having the kind of vitality that overflows.

5. **Self-love is the foundation that determines how strongly we can give and receive love.** Without it, our relationships will crumble under the slightest storm. Take the responsibility for understanding your fears and needs, and for facing them in a loving way.

6. **Self-love rests on self-forgiveness.** It entails being able to understand who we were when we failed ourselves and what needs, hurts, fears, and deprivations were driving us. Only then may we meet ourselves with compassion and kindness. This is why our growth in self-understanding brings healing and reconciliation with our essential selves.

7. **Self-love is learning how to be tough with ourselves.** It is the ability to take the driver's seat in our life when we need to break a destructive mood or habit. We must remember that being tough with ourselves means being committed and energetic, having tenacity and high standards. Being tough with ourselves is the opposite of being hard on ourselves,

which means being perfectionistic, self-critical, self-punishing, and unable to accept our mistakes and weaknesses. It is important for us to remember each day that to embody love, to be love, begins with a foundation of self-love and self-compassion.

Love, as you can easily imagine from reading these steps, takes courage. As the pandemic and economic and political chaos keep staring us in the face, we must remember that, throughout history, having courage of heart is one of our noblest virtues. Facing this journey we have been thrust into, we must turn it into a quest by having the courage to learn and seek. Even if we become seekers as a result of desperation, we can and must find courage within ourselves, because it is so easy to fall into despair, bitterness, and helplessness in the face of difficulties.

Courage enables us to look into the darkness in our lives and in ourselves and to search for the light of new meaning, new purpose, and new directions, including the path to grow beyond our current situation. When we love ourselves, when we feel the love and support deep within us, we find the courage and the energy to imagine new things, new lives. The experience of being loved creates in us the desire to be transformed. We undergo a softening toward and an increased awareness of others. And we must remember that love always takes the risk of birth, no matter what state the world is in.

In the end of *The Fire Next Time,* Baldwin imagined that relatively conscious Whites and relatively conscious people of color could lovingly create new consciousness in others and change the trajectory of the world. And, he said, we must dare everything. True self-love is the foundation of outrageous love that gives hope, purpose, and direction to a re-imagined future and the courage to dare everything for it.

Thoughts and Questions to Ponder

- While you were reading this section, I shared with you that "when I was young, I thought self-love was the most natural thing in the world. But it is not. With maturity, I learned better. Self-interest and self-denial may seem natural, but they are more likely driven by our complexes and wounded hearts. Self-love is another story. Self-love is one of the most difficult things in the world to achieve." Can you make a list of all of the ways you find self-love hard to achieve?

- What do you think of my using Rogers's approach to the therapeutic relationship—being genuinely engaged, emotionally congruent, warm, and sympathetic, as well as unconditional positive regard—as the first steps on my own path to self-love?

- As you read these principles and reflect on them, respond to each one by writing in your journal.

- What does it mean to you that "love always takes the risk of birth, no matter what state the world is in"? It may be helpful to reread the next-to-last paragraph in this section, which ends with the above reminder.

Other Thoughts?

Lesson Seven

Love Must Be Strong

Love is strong, and must be recognized as strong; it must be willing to roar. Analyst Dr. James Hillman writes in his essays *The Thought of the Heart, and, The Soul of the World* that when young lions are born, they must be awakened with a roar. He tells us the young lions need to be awakened in our hearts. He writes, "What is passive, immobile, asleep in the heart creates a desert which can only be cured by its own parenting principle that shows its awakening care by roaring…. The more our desert, the more we must rage, which rage is love." These thoughts leave me wondering, "Can we ever again become wholly what we are meant to be?"

For years, my writing has sought to understand what is happening to our society, to us, and to me. I believe my first task is to see and accept reality. Then I must seek to understand it from a personal perspective. Failing to understand the truth of our experiences individually and collectively is the surest guarantee of increasing strife that will assault the well-being of every one of us. Failing to understand the challenges we face will cause us to pay a dear price in our innermost lives as well as in the spirit of our country. I think I have made it clear throughout that facing our reality and seeking to understand it does not mean that we take on an attitude of permitting or acquiescing to anything. Accepting and understanding reality is the necessary foundation that will help us face the apocalypse we are in today, create a whole new life for ourselves and our society, and quit paying the price of our ignorance in blood.

My reflections bring to mind a talk that Dr. Philip Hallie gave titled "Cruelty: The Empirical Evil" at a symposium on "Facing Evil" (in a book with the same title), put together by Jungian analyst Dr. Harry Wilmer in the mid-1980s. Hallie was a well-known author and the Griffin Professor of Philosophy and Humanities at Wesleyan University in Middletown, Connecticut. A World War II veteran, he became intrigued with the story of Le Chambon, a small French mountain village that devoted itself during the war to rescuing refugees from the Nazis—at the risk of the villagers' lives. Hallie was so moved by this story that he incorporated it into a book that became an international bestseller. At the time, the village exemplified for Hallie the power of love.

But as time passed, he began to feel that something in his heart resented this village. He said, "They didn't stop Hitler. They did nothing to stop Hitler…A thousand Le Chambons would not have stopped Hitler. It took decent murderers like me to do it. Murderers who had compunctions, but murdered nonetheless…The cruelty that I perpetrated willingly was the only way to stop the cruel march that I and others like me were facing." Hallie received three Battle Stars while serving with the famous 82nd Airborne Division of the U.S. Army in Europe during World War II.

The fact that Dr. Hallie had to become a murderer and perpetuate cruelty to defeat evil should teach us a bitter lesson. That lesson is that when we don't love life and each other enough to follow the ethical imperative, "to do what is right and just," we open the door for the powerful forces of evil to step in. Then like Dr. Hallie we run the risk of having to take on another form of evil to combat the evil we are facing. Our most urgent reason for becoming love warriors is to overcome the growing power of evil without another form of evil taking its place.

Hallie's story reminds me again that the great social psychoanalyst Erich Fromm, in his book *The Anatomy of Human Destructiveness,* defined two kinds of aggression: malignant and benign. Malignant aggression destroys life. Benign aggression is used in the service of life. When we are called to face the malignant aggression in our lives—in our politics, our society, our cities, our families, and within ourselves—it is a call to use a force of will, assertion, and commitment. In other words, we must use the power of the outrageous love of life against the forces destroying life. We are in this world to be healers, listeners, servants, and lovers. We are also here to be creators and spiritual warriors.

A few years ago, there was a lot of social discourse about people living in a bubble. In too many cases, too many of us had remained conveniently ignorant of cruelties in our society, and some of us even regarded this ignorance as a virtue. On many levels we experienced innocent naiveté, or willful naiveté. Consequently, we neither saw nor understood the cruelty we were personally and collectively participating in. In fact, I now consider willful naiveté and willful ignorance to be malicious aggression because they destroy life-affirming opportunities at both the individual and the societal levels. In every chapter in my book *The Midnight Hour*, I am straightforward about the cruelties in our society to people all around us, and even to ourselves, that we need to wake up to.

The people who scare me the most are the "good people." The ones theologian Reinhold Niebuhr was referring to when he said, "Most evil is not done by evil people, but by good people who don't know what they are doing." Good people who are willfully naive may attend religious services, give money to charities, collect clothes for people who are homeless, or spend their holidays serving food to people who are food insecure. "Good people" decry violence, listen to impassioned sermons, go to adult forums and lectures on spirituality. But here are the real questions: Will they do anything to change the dark issues revealed in our apocalypse? Will they step out of their comfort zones and imagined security to stop the predators trying to take over our government? In his great book *Strength to Love*, Martin Luther King, Jr. warned us that sincerity and conscientiousness are not enough. Will they/we/I love life enough to become outrageously fierce in the service of life?

Unfortunately, people who were raised in the White pseudo-Christian middle-class, as I was, were taught prejudices that are great stumbling blocks to the ability to be aggressive in the service of life. We were trained to be *nice*, to avoid anger, not to mention to avoid acting in anger (much less in outrage). We were even taught that expressing ourselves clearly and directly is considered aggressive or confrontational. In essence, we were taught that to be kind and loving is to be passive and pleasing.

We need to awaken and love life dearly. As I write these words, I am reminded of a story I've used in my books and lectures. It is an old story about

Saint Francis and the wolf. The story has helped me develop a sense of comfort, even affection, with the savage side of myself. The tale takes place a long time ago when there were still vast forests in Italy. The people in a small village began to notice that some of their chickens and livestock were disappearing. Then, tragically, some children and older people went missing. As the villagers put together a few clues—bloody bits of fur, signs of struggles, and paw prints—they realized a ferocious wolf had moved into the nearby woods.

Animals and weaker people were customary prey, but the wolf seemed to be getting increasingly bold. The villagers tried in vain to poison, capture, or kill the wolf, but they were unable to even find it. They called for hunters from near and far to kill it. Elegant nobles with great horses, packs of hounds, and many retainers tried to help the villagers. But the wolf evaded them all.

Eventually the village elders, in desperation, sent a message to Saint Francis. Saint Francis came immediately to their aid. He arrived at the village and plunged into the forest, without pausing to eat or rest. He journeyed deeper into the dense vegetation than anyone had gone before, searching for the wolf's lair. In the dim light of a small clearing, he found the wolf. They stood before each other, eye to eye, for some time. Finally, Saint Francis said simply, "Brother wolf."

When Saint Francis returned to the village, the excited people gathered around him and begged him to tell them how to deal with the wolf. He said to them, "Feed your wolf."

It is important to realize that in the symbolism of this story none of the conventional means of power shown by the villagers, nobles, or hunters were effective in eliminating the wolf. Symbolically, this means that denial, repression, and will power will not enable us to control the instinctual power within us. Saint Francis as the image of love and spirit is what is called for. The interaction between Saint Francis and the wolf shows us that love and spirit must recognize the deep capacity for fierceness within us and be in relationship with it to keep us from destroying ourselves.

The lesson in this story is simple. We must face our capacity for fierceness. To feed our capacity for fierceness means we honor it with conscious awareness and integrate it into our personalities as part of our journey into wholeness. Feeding our wolf is necessary to give us the strength not only to support a life of love and responsibility but also to respond to personal and social problems with caring and competence. These responses must honor our tradition of human dignity, the sacredness of each person, and our ideal of a community in which people help one another.

Learn to believe that love must be outrageously strong and have purpose and direction. Outrageous love must be passionate and creative. Love, in its most authentic form, understands that our current national condition of cruelty hides under the guise of not being "aggressive." This is a form of extremism that will disgrace us through generations far into the future.

This type of love requires sacrifice, meaning that we must learn to love the lives of others as well as our own. This type of love makes it clear that comfort can quickly become its own corruption. When we love beyond our own lives and comfort, we begin to love the lives of those connected to us, and we are challenged and inspired to build a better world for all of us.

When we don't confront reality and the cruelties being inflicted by our societal shadows, we set ourselves up to pay a terrible price. If we don't personally and collectively embrace the changes we need to make for the evolution of our consciousness and social awareness, I believe the price we pay will be in blood. Jung also believed this, as illustrated in his writings in *Civilization in Transition* (CW, vol. 10), and Hallie expresses this in his writings as well. In fact, we have paid this price in blood for some time. However, if we take the risks and face the challenges of change and transformation that are clearly beckoning us, we will invite the breath of life to renew us and to open our minds, hearts, and lives to a whole new life together. Loving authentically means using every single means at our disposal to pursue and enhance our values of life, liberty, opportunity, equality, and justice for all.

As you can likely see, writing these words brings into focus for me the fact that outrageous love demands clarity, passion, and action. Yet, I still wonder if I have written enough.

Thoughts and Questions to Ponder

- Love must be strong. Love must be willing to roar. Love must be as fierce as a wolf. Love must be willing to fight for life and must exist in the service of life. Write out for yourself how these descriptions of love match up with how you were taught to define love and a loving life.

- What was your response to my statement that denial in the form of willful naiveté and ignorance are malicious aggression because they destroy the life-affirming opportunities for individuals and for society?

- Did it make sense to you when you read "The people who scare me the most are the 'good people'"?

- Can you list comforts that have become corruptions in your life?

- Can you now write a summary of what strong love means to you?

Other Thoughts?

Lesson Eight

Healing Alienation is Crucial

As I write about alienation, I realize I am in an interesting place. During the last few years, I have found myself, as a Jungian analyst, deeply involved with people who are responding to the suffering, fear, chaos, and uncertainty of these times. I too feel these things and I am threatened by them. I have felt overwhelmed at times by the anger, anxiety, pain, and confusion of the times we are living in. Yet, I am also filled with a profound and abiding gratitude for the life I have, the experiences in my Jungian journey, and being able to help facilitate the journey in other people's lives. "Gratitude" is a word I cherish along with the word "compassion." Both of these words help define the foundation of what it means to be human for me. And I believe the meanings of these words are born from the love within our hearts.

We are at a crucial turning point in our history. The core issue challenging our culture is **alienation**.

It is at the root of decades of increasing violence, destruction for destruction's sake in our politics, too many newscasts, uncivil internet communications, and a scattered, non-cohesive response to the pandemic.

It is helpful to remember that the first way to empower ourselves and our future is to confront our reality. Then I think it is helpful to ask ourselves: "What is our legacy going to be? How will future generations remember us?" This period, the days passing right now, are going to be judged and judged severely in practical, spiritual, and moral terms by history unless we create fundamental changes in the values our society stands for. Our failure to live peaceably in our families, communities, cities, states, and nation points out our self-delusions of power, success, positive thinking, and individualism. We are no longer able to deny that there is much rage, fear, violence, and alienation. As we begin to confront the realities behind our alienation, we should remember that Dr. Jung wrote: "One does not become enlightened by imagining figures of light, but by making the darkness conscious."

What is alienation? Etymologically, the word means "estrangement." "It is the state or experience of being isolated from a group or activity to which one should belong or in which one should be involved."

Most of us have tried to live a good enough life to feel a certain amount of security and self-satisfaction. But today our society is like the proverbial frog sitting in a slowly heating pot of water that will eventually boil and kill it. Because the temperature is rising slowly, the frog doesn't realize it needs to jump out of the pot. Like the frog, we have lived for decades in a society where the temperature of our toxic stress has been rising.

The fear comes from threats to our well-being that seem beyond our control. The threats may be to our security, our identities, our place and value in our culture. Losses can bring shame and threaten our self-worth, our health, and even the safety of our loved ones. Like the hot frog, we are trying to adjust to a now dangerous situation that is incrementally dehumanizing us and can destroy our lives.

As these threats, stresses, and fears increase, they estrange us—they alienate us—from our neighbors, from our experience of being a valued citizen, and from being part of a nation we feel loyal to. They alienate us from the history of what was once considered our greatest strength—our ability to stand up to any challenge no matter how difficult. But, even more important, they alienate us from our hearts, the source of our capacities for courage, love, and compassion.

Well over a half century ago we experienced

the first mass shooting of fourteen people at the University of Texas Tower in Austin, by a lone shooter. The shock of this event motivated two of our greatest social psychoanalysts, Dr. Erich Fromm and Dr. Rolla May, to extensively study what was taking place in our society to produce such a horrible event. They asked: what was taking place in our society, not just in the shooter?

Both doctors came to the same conclusion: if we become dehumanized to the point of feeling alienated from self and others, we become filled with profound inner rage and compelled to be destructive. In that state we can easily be manipulated by media and political influences that focus our rage and fear on supposed enemies—personal, political and institutional.

Dehumanization, alienation, and rage have been building in our society like the heat being turned up around the frog in the pot. Unlike the frog, we can at this moment become aware of our danger, our pain, and the increasing sources of alienation. The pain, the challenges, and the destructive tendencies are not discomforts we should deny, bemoan, or turn away from. They are calling us to awaken to spiritual growth, "to love our neighbor as ourselves." We must also remember that **hope** comes from taking responsibility and being engaged, especially in uncomfortable times.

Thoughts and Questions to Ponder

I would like to ask you to follow Jung's advice to look into your and our darkness through these questions:

- What are your thoughts about dehumanization and alienation taking place in our society today, and perhaps in yourself? Are you willing to discuss these powerful emotions and their effects with friends and family members?

- Is it easier to deny their existence? How can you accept the challenge to begin the conversation to bring these powerful forces into the light, to turn the heat off on the stove?

- How can you, as a human being, be changed by accepting this challenge?

- And please remember that knowledge, especially self-knowledge, brings help and hope and the ability to re-imagine ourselves and our futures.

Other Thoughts?

Lesson Nine

Cultivating Compassion

Revitalizing compassion is an interesting term to me. To revitalize means to take something that is deteriorating and inject new life into it. The true definition of *compassion* is "to suffer with" or "to suffer together." Well, while I was brought up to think being compassionate is a virtue, I was taught practically nothing about what it might mean other than empathy or pity. Of course, empathy and pity are not suffering with or feeling with. Extending empathy or pity rarely creates/reflects any real understanding of the life experiences and circumstances of the other person or group of people.

The British religious writer Karen Armstrong tells us in her memoir, *The Spiral Staircase: My Climb Out of Darkness*, that she discovered that "the theme of compassion...is pivotal to all of the great religious traditions...at their best."

"I have been in and out of churches for decades

and have not encountered compassion, 'suffering with', as a central theme in their Sunday teachings," she writes. "Yet, as I have read the New Testament, it seems to me that to feed the hungry, give drink to the thirsty, welcome the stranger, clothe the naked, visit the sick, and write to the prisoner are in some form the general theme in every sermon of Jesus. Further, he says in Matthew 25:20, 'I tell you solemnly, in so far as you did this to the least of these brothers [and sisters] of mine you did it to me.' With these words he makes compassion a sacred activity. I wonder what has happened to those of us who call ourselves Christians and how we can all begin to become what our great religions are calling us to become."

Jung gives us a starting point to revitalize the strength of compassion within ourselves. In *Collected Works* (vol. 11, para. 520-521), he writes that accepting ourselves with compassion is the first journey we must make. This point of view puts a whole new slant on how we were taught about compassion in the past. It challenges us in a more personal and profound way. We must suffer with ourselves, and seek out the beggar, the enemy, the stranger, and the criminal within ourselves. We must not preach but reflect. We must seek out those parts of ourselves that we condemn, rage against, hide from the world, and strike from our awareness. We must be able to "give them the alms of our own kindness," seek not to embrace them but to understand them with compassion. This practice brings true humility to us, and as this journey continues, we learn more about how to live with wisdom so that the practice of inner compassion flows outward.

In my lectures and writings, I have described this approach to the journey of cultivating compassion as the "Descent into Life." When I have written and spoken about this journey, I've always found it interesting, even amusing, that when the newest pied piper for enlightenment is speaking in our town, he or she is usually focusing on how we can achieve peace and joy. Well, no wonder! That is what sells and what creates followings, because that is what so many of us think we are longing for.

On the other hand, as Armstrong points out, all of our great religions (and I am not speaking of the pied pipers they also have)—those that religious scholar Huston Smith calls our wisdom traditions—have a very different emphasis. For example, a rabbi famous in Jewish history lived in a tent pitched next to the walls of Jerusalem because he wanted to be close to the poor. When Siddhārtha walked out of his father's palace, he came face-to-face with poverty, illness, and death. These encounters launched his journey into becoming the Buddha. In Christianity, Jesus says in the gospel of Matthew, "For I have come to call not the righteous but sinners," when he was asked about the people he liked to spend his time with.

Our wisdom traditions tell us that the root meaning of the word *salvation* is "the way of redemption" or "the way to wholeness." As we follow this line of thinking, we discover that our journey into wholeness, or "holiness" in the words of the mystical traditions, begins in a paradoxical way—not by a search for peace and joy but by acknowledging the grit and grist of life: suffering, illness, death, and our alienation from ourselves and the depth of our own spiritual and psychological capacities. In other words, our journey begins with learning the meaning of compassion through our own experiences. Now, this is a very important point: it is the full acceptance of these aspects of ourselves that initiates our journey into becoming fully human, fully incarnated, and more open to joy.

Of course, we all want a good life. And when we encounter life's difficulties, we want to quickly restore our peace of mind and good relationships, *and* we want to keep our lifestyle and habits—the personalities we are used to. And, of course, our culture supports this point of view. The culture doesn't see our wounds and difficulties as calls for transformation. It sees them as symptoms to alleviate so we can get back to "normal," which actually means functional in a social way, not a spiritual, psychological, or even a personally fulfilling way.

Furthermore, most of us envision a life that is successful, prosperous, and fulfilling, and if we have children, we dream of a successful life for them. We get angry with ourselves and with life when our dreams and visions don't come true. But the failure of these dreams and visions to manifest themselves is very important, for it is meant to awaken us to compassion—compassion not only for others but for ourselves and for how difficult life is.

Generally, we need our dreams of a good life to carry us into adulthood. But, later, we also need for these dreams to fail, in order to make way for our wholeness to begin to emerge and be discovered. And we need the self-compassion that these experiences can generate, in order to accept the difficulties in our lives as spiritual and psychological incubations and not as failures. Further, as we begin the work that Jung called "the realization of our shadow," we need this capacity for compassion in order to accept the poor, dispossessed, and disapproved part of ourselves.

> To illustrate this point, I'll share with you the words of the Ba'al Shem Ṭov, founder of the Hasidic tradition in Judaism. He said, "There are many rooms in God's castle." Does that sound familiar? He then went on to say, "There is, however,

one key that opens every room, and that
key is a broken heart."

We need to have the courage and love to engage
in life enough to have our hearts broken. Such broken hearts are not signs of failure. Rather, they open
us to compassion and to becoming more fully human. These experiences not only humble us but also
compel us to become aware of and outgrow our former selves and worldview.

Compassion, in its true sense, is the acceptance
that life is full of difficulties and suffering. Accepting
this reality and our ability to be in it, suffering with
and caring about each other, brings us to the highest spiritual potentials in all of the great religions.
Along with courage and love, compassion is a key
ingredient to creating a fulfilling life for a person
and for a culture. Again, I want to share with you
seven principles I have used in my life, teaching, and
writings to help cultivate compassion within ourselves, one day at a time.

1. **Compassion is difficult** because the way
   we usually think of it is as an ideal, seen
   from a distance. We prefer to assume we
   are compassionate even though we have
   not accepted our own suffering, responding
   to it instead with a fight or flight reaction.
   It might be helpful for you to review your

thoughts about compassion. Why do you think we should become compassionate? Do you think making this journey to crack our hearts open is worthwhile?

2. **Acceptance of suffering** reminds us that what we need is self-compassion, not self-judgment. Remember that acceptance is the necessary first step in transforming anything psychological. Our suffering may be caused by events, people, illnesses, inner conflicts, or the early or even later traumas in our life. But the healing path and our capacity to grow through and beyond our circumstances—that is, to transform our suffering—begins with self-compassion. Our compassion for ourselves is a cornerstone for having compassion for others.

3. **We must value the inhabitants of our shadow,** the parts of ourselves that we have disowned, devalued, rejected, and repressed. The great poet Rilke reminds us that "perhaps all the dragons of our lives are princesses who are only waiting to see us act, just once, with beauty and courage. Perhaps everything that frightens us is, in its deepest essence, something helpless that needs our love." This means getting to know and understand—remember

this doesn't mean embracing—some of our most negative feelings and self-critical voices. Journaling is very helpful not only for engaging in this step but for developing all of these principles. Keep in mind, nothing in our shadows scares us more, or needs our self-compassion more, than our own denied and impoverished potentials.

4. **Compassion is in our nature.** We are born helpless, but ready to love and be loved. This reality means compassion is a basic part of our nature. We need to be cared for and we need to care for others. Unfortunately, in this time, we have developed a power-driven, achievement-oriented culture that wants us to adopt its values of success, rather than living by the values of the human heart. One of these is compassion for ourselves and others, as our great religions teach us. If we stop to think about it for a minute, we might wonder how we can be shocked at the rage, conflict, and alienation that has been erupting in our society over a long time.

5. **Compassion calls for action.** By *action*, I mean becoming sensitive to the needs of our own hearts and those of others. It is helpful to define what we think are compassionate

actions toward ourselves and others. I've named some for you to consider in these principles. Once you have a list for yourself, see if you can convert it into a list of practices to follow day by day. Repeated practices lead us to cultivate a new awareness as our hearts are born anew into how we are living.

6. **Compassion creates openness.** To be compassionate to ourselves means being open to our shadow. We may be shocked and surprised to find more pain dwelling there than we imagined. The same is true when looking into our societal shadow. Developing compassion is a lifelong process because the more we develop the light of awareness, the more darkness is revealed. While this process may be startling at times, it should not be discouraging. As we do this work, more human potentials in ourselves and in our society will come into our conscious awareness. Take responsibility for understanding this process and for facing it in a curious, compassionate way.

7. **Have compassion for your enemies,** within and without. In her book *Twelve Steps to a Compassionate Life,* Karen Armstrong's final step is "Love Your Enemies." She isn't naive or sentimental about this step. She advises us to

"look carefully and deeply into our own hearts and thus learn to see the sorrow of our enemy." She is talking about an enemy with a capital *E*, something or someone that seems to threaten our survival and everything we stand for, as these troubling times are doing. We must keep in mind that compassion is a heart response. It seeks to suffer together and also to understand.

Neither of these actions means to acquiesce to or embrace. The first act of compassion is to seek to understand. Failing to understand an enemy within or outside of ourselves, personally and collectively, is the guarantee of mounting strife.

True compassion takes both love and courage. I hope that from this brief look into compassion you will find that you can cultivate it, no matter how discouraged you might feel at times. Viktor Frankl in his great book about surviving the Nazi concentration camps, *Man's Search for Meaning,* writes that prisoners with compassion could reach beyond themselves to help others experience a humanity that made them feel that life had meaning and was endurable. The more we cultivate courage, love, and compassion in our lives, the better able we are to choose our responses in any given circumstances, to choose our own way, and even to become strong defenders of the values of the heart, of life.

Thoughts and Questions to Ponder

Compassion, as I have pointed out, is not a term too many of us have a personal relationship with. Karen Armstrong points out, however, that it is a major premise of most of the great religions. Can you write a personal response to what I have written about Jung's starting point for revitalizing compassion in our personal lives? His statement is reprinted below.

> Jung gives us the starting point for revitalizing the strength of compassion within ourselves. In *Collected Works* (vol. 11, para. 520-521), he writes that accepting ourselves with compassion is the first journey we must make. This point of view puts a whole new slant on how we were taught about compassion in the past. It challenges us in a more personal and profound way. We must suffer with ourselves, and seek out the beggar, the enemy, the stranger, and the criminal within ourselves. We must not preach but reflect. We must seek out those parts of ourselves that we condemn, rage against, hide from the world, and strike from our awareness. We must be able to "give them the alms of our own kindness," seek not to embrace them but to

understand them with compassion. This practice brings true humility to us, and as this journey continues, we learn more about how to live with wisdom so that the practice of inner compassion flows outward.

- As you explore more about compassion and yourself, respond in your journal to these lines I wrote: "We need to have the courage and love to engage in life enough to have our hearts broken. Such broken hearts are not signs of failure. Rather, they open us to compassion and to becoming more fully human. These experiences not only humble us but also compel us to become aware of and outgrow our former selves and worldview. Compassion, in its true sense, is the acceptance that life is full of difficulties and suffering. Accepting this reality and our ability to be in it, suffering with and caring about each other, brings us to the highest spiritual potentials in all of the great religions." Please take your time and explore the reality behind these statements.

- How have you been taught to think and feel about your own suffering?

- These seven principles for cultivating compassion are not commonly included in the perspective on life we are taught as we grow up. I invite you to journal about each one and the feelings, thoughts, and personal experiences they bring up in you.

- List some of your enemies within and without, including some of your perceived political and societal enemies. Can you begin to see the humanity, fear, sorrow, sources of anger, and other human characteristics in them?

Other Thoughts?

Accepting the Challenges
of the Heart

The troubling times we are in are real and, as I pointed out, have many layers. They are a dark revelation of what our future will become if we fail to recognize the sacredness of every person and of all life. The pandemic, with so many terrible deaths, and the violence and anger in our society expose how passive we have become in regard to the sacredness of life. It also shows us the strength with which some of us can deny the imminent possibility of the death of ourselves, those we care about, and even our planet.

These troubling times are also unveiling harsh realities that have long existed in our lives and our society. It shows, as Armstrong notes in her books, that we haven't seen clearly enough that we all live in one world. Jung and most Jungian scholars and analysts agree with this perspective. When our shortsighted approaches to living and our value structures exclude and dispossess parts of ourselves and parts of humanity, they will come back to haunt us in destructive forms. And the belief that we can isolate ourselves from this reality is an illusion.

The challenges we are facing mean we cannot go back to how we were before. Our previous state, incidentally, was not safe and secure, because it was sustaining the festering problems that now confront us.

We are faced with challenges that have no easy answers. Even the effort to fully understand them requires a collective transformation, a change in the heart of our social character. Since the 1970s we have developed a pattern of seeking quick solutions and appearing successful. We apply Band-Aid fixes to crises by treating symptoms, rather than search-ing for the more profound causes of our difficulties. If we try to follow this old pattern, the appearance of success will become more important than trans-formation, than revitalizing courage, love, and com-passion. If we succumb to the compulsion to pursue successful appearances, we lose our ability to truly get to know ourselves, the depth of other people, and the nature of the crisis we are in. The secret here is that if enough people transform their hearts, then our society can truly change for the better.

We are challenged through love and courage to transform ourselves and the heart of our society. To accept this challenge, we must have the courage to live with fear, anxiety, loss, and an unknown future that is actually filled with great potentials. Accepting this challenge means fully choosing life and choosing to live not only with courage but also with love and compassion, which will become strength and realism in a very profound way. We now face challenges both personally and collectively. Our main concern must be with creating a different understanding of who we can be, personally and together. Through this understanding, we can cultivate the ability and the will to create a new beginning for this country.

The Jungian position is that if we can make the needed transformation within ourselves, we can lessen and more effectively deal with the threatening external events we face. In some cases we may even solve our most pressing problems. If a sufficient number of people can experience transformation—by having a change of heart that brings the focus of life away from power and back to love—we may be spared the worst possibilities of what now faces us.

The big picture is now in our hands. If we love life, ourselves, and the people who are dear to us, we must become love warriors.

Thoughts and Questions to Ponder

- Reading this book has been a short but intense journey for most readers. I invite you to sit back, let its contents simmer in your mind, and then write about what comes up in your thoughts and feelings. Consider discussing them with people you feel comfortable with.

• You might also note questions that come up for you that I haven't covered or thought about.

Appendix

Helpful Practices for the Journey

At the end of each part in this book, I invited you to use two of the three techniques I describe in my book, *Sacred Selfishness*, as my spiritual practices. I call them my spiritual practices because I've learned that following them religiously continuously transforms my life for the better. They are journaling as a means of reflection, befriending dreams, and active imagination. I am including two brief sections in this appendix that explain more about my approaches to journaling and dreamwork. I hope that you find them as helpful, exciting, and transforming as I have.

Journaling Suggestions

From *Sacred Selfishness*, pp. 154-156
Important Elements in Personal Journal Writing

- Privacy ensures trust and provides a space where we can encounter our many aspects truthfully.

- Self-understanding comes from writing down honestly who we are today within the context of our lives.

- Our journals become concrete records over time: studying them can reveal psychological patterns in our lives.

- Examining relationships, feelings, and interactions can be a source for discovering features of ourselves we have denied.

- Including our reflections in our personal journals leads to self-confrontation and to a new consciousness.

In our journals we should include our dreams and our thoughts and responses to them. As we're reflecting on the events we've recorded, we can write down any new insights, feelings, and other ideas or material that come to mind. A journal is a good place to examine the feelings and behaviors we had during the day, or the feelings we didn't get a chance to express.

Writing down a description of each situation where we think we feel a particular emotion can often help us get a better understanding of what's happening. For example, one man I know felt resentment whenever his wife suggested he might need a coat, a hat, an umbrella, or something else when he left the house. He thought she was treating him like a child. As he wrote about these situations, he became aware that she might be expressing her care for him and he was "hearing her like a child" whose mother was chiding him. With this insight he was then able to accept and appreciate her love for him.

Journal-keeping is both a personal workbook and an intensely personal form of self-expression. As such, it has no right or wrong format. All that matters is that you find a format that works for you, that fits your personality, and that can grow and change with you. Some people I know use elegant notebooks while others use a computer disk. I've always been the most comfortable with the kind of spiral notebooks I used in college.

Normal journaling takes about ten or fifteen minutes a day unless you're exploring something intensely. Then you may take longer, but rarely will you write for more than thirty minutes. People often ask me how they should handle dreams, and I advise them to write the dreams down immediately, whether it is during the night or first thing in the morning. Spouses, lovers, and other people in your home often have to learn to gracefully allow you some time with yourself before you start the day. In many circumstances dreamwork attracts interest, and the other people around you might start paying more attention to their own dreams.

Journaling is a particularly good way of reflecting at the end of the day, and many people do it before going to sleep. The time of the day or the length of time you devote to journaling, however, can be worked out to fit your own pattern as long as you treat the practice with respect rather than as something you try to force into your schedule. You may take days off here and there to keep your journaling fresh, so that it does not become routine and mechanical. Your inner work has its own inner substance—this is the beginning, where you launch the journey deep within yourself.

Tips for Journal Writing

- Record what is going on or what has happened inside of you as well as outside.

- Make special note of strong emotional reactions during the day.

- Reflect on these reactions, and on the situations and relationships in which they occurred.

- Record thoughts, ideas, fantasies, and dreams.

- Try to simply reflect on dreams and see what they bring to mind.

- Record events that surround dreams and see if they seem related to you.

- Record drawings, poetry, quotations, and whatever else comes to mind.

- Record your personal fantasies and ambitions for both the present and the future.

In the foreword of her lovely and inspiring book *Gift from the Sea,* Anne Morrow Lindbergh explains how the book began as a journal "in order to think out my own particular pattern of living, my own individual balance of life, work and human relationships." She discovered through her writing and by talking about her writing with other people, that once she looked beneath the surface of life, many men and women in various circumstances and in many forms were "grappling with essentially the same questions." We are all seeking the sense of security that arrives when we have learned to become more intimate with ourselves. Journaling helps us find assurance that the creativity, values, and ideals that arise inside of us are gifts we can nurture and develop. And when we have found out how to listen to ourselves, we are able to act with strength, greet the world with joy, and share our gifts with others.

Dreams as Friends

From *Sacred Selfishness*, pp. 224-229

True friendship is both an art and a craft. Friendships may often seem to begin easily, but their nature is delicate at first; growth is slow and is easily checked or diverted. For friendships to become strong they need to be nurtured, cultivated, and appreciated. Few of us are born with a natural gift for cultivating friendships. They take time, caring, and mutual respect. And the busyness that devours our lives makes enriching our friendships difficult. But once a friendship has become strong, it's very sturdy and reliable. A real friend can tell us things we don't want to tell ourselves, and yet we're always comforted to know there's someone out there we can lean on.

Some years ago, the writer Sophie Loeb said, "A friend is one who withholds judgment no matter how long you have his unanswered letter." These characteristics of friendships explain why befriending the dream is an idea that makes immediate sense to most of us. It's much more comforting to feel that our inner lives are friendly toward us even if they're provoking us with dramatic images or confronting our preferred opinions.

In therapy it's tempting for both the therapist and the patient to translate dreams into their favorite theories, perspectives, or rationalizations. In many of these situations, dream interpretations are used to dredge up childhood conflicts or to gain information, power, or energy from our unconscious to help us pursue our goals. Yet these approaches are actually hostile to our unconscious. They go against the grain of friendships, for nothing damages a friendship more than trying to exploit it. Unfortunately, modern therapies are often influenced by the social character of our times, which emphasizes solving problems in order to become more functional, rather than honoring our inner lives so that we can become more whole as human beings. When the fruits of friendship and the cultivation of our inner lives and wisdom aren't valued, therapy can actually work against our healing and growth and contribute to devaluing life.

The beauty of befriending dreams is that it doesn't require special knowledge and training. It simply asks that we *listen* to what they have to say to us and appreciate their importance.

Paying Attention

Paying attention to our dream lives involves several activities. To begin with, it's beneficial if we can create favorable conditions for receiving our dreams. An overextended schedule, exhaustion, poor sleeping habits, and the general habit of just being too busy can distract us from the quality time we commit to our dreams, or for that matter to any friendship. Making an effort to create an attitude of interest and receptivity by trying to have a good night's sleep and waking up gently very likely will invite a response from our unconscious.

The second way of paying attention to dreams is to write them down as soon as we wake up. It's better not to put them off until morning, if we remember them in the middle of the night, or to wait until after we've had coffee and are dressed. Time and experience have proven that until this friendship is firmly established, no matter how often we go over a dream in our minds, we can lose it in a moment if we haven't written it down.

Research proves we dream every night. If we don't remember the contents of our dreams, it usually means we're overtired, anxious, or have some other trouble keeping us from concentrating on our inner lives. Having a pencil and paper available nearby and writing dreams down quickly is a helpful ritual that stimulates our memory of them. When we wake up and don't remember a dream, lying quietly and focusing on what we have been thinking since we awakened can be helpful. Perhaps a thought or an image, a mood, an impression about ourselves in some past action, or thinking about the future will come to mind. Writing these thoughts down can revive or recall others, jump-starting a train of thinking that can lead to reconstructing a dream.

I've often awakened in the morning and been surprised by the number of dreams I wrote down during the night with no memory of even writing them. At other times, when I only recall a brief scene, I've discovered that writing it down carefully may help the entire dream return to memory. A short time ago I remembered the image of a brown bear from a dream. As I was writing a detailed description of the bear, the dream story began returning and eventually covered three pages.

And now we come to the third important aspect of paying attention to a dream, which is to write it down with all the detail you can. Recording it carefully helps you to see or feel the full development of the dream. And describing the moods, people, animals, landscapes, and actions in lively ways helps you re-imagine the dream as a story that you can experience again.

In his delightful and wise book, *The Star Thrower*, anthropologist Loren Eiseley shares a dream in a manner that pulls us directly into it:

> The dream was of a great blurred bear-like shape emerging from the snow against the window. It pounded on the glass and beckoned importunately toward the forest. I caught the urgency of a message as uncouth and indecipherable as the shape of its huge bear in the snow. In the immense terror of my dream, I struggled against the import of that message as I struggled also to resist the impatient pounding of the frost-enveloped beast at the window.

Suddenly I lifted the telephone beside my bed, and through the receiver came a message miraculous in origin. For I knew intuitively, in the still snowfall of my dream, that the voice I heard, a long way off, was my own voice in childhood. Pure and sweet, incredibly refined and beautiful beyond the things of earth, yet somehow inexorable and not to be stayed, the voice was already terminating its messages. "I am sorry to have troubled you," the clear faint syllables of the child persisted. They seemed to come across a thinning wire that lengthened far away into the years of my past. "I am sorry, I am sorry to have troubled you at all." The voice faded before I could speak. I was awake now, trembling in the cold.

As I read this dream, I feel like I do when I read a good poem—left with a sense of wonder. Most of us have to relearn how to express ourselves in such a complete manner.

Julia Cameron, in *The Right to Write*, offers useful advice in this direction by urging us to become what she calls "bad writers." By this phrase she means letting everything be expressed even if we think we're describing feelings and events in tabloid terms, where beauties are breathtaking, villains hideous, victims helpless, and murders grisly. We've been so schooled to censor ourselves, putting down "just the facts." When we do this, we can end up losing the poetry and flavor of our dreams, like someone who stops digging in a hollow tree a few inches before reaching the honey.

Listening

Listening to the dream includes writing it down as completely as we remember it and including its colorful aspects. However, we must keep in mind that listening to a dream is similar to what we do when we *really* want someone to listen to us. We want them to put aside their agendas, their censoring mind-sets, and their "plans" to answer us. This is why I like to tell people that while writing the dream down, they should suspend the temptation to interpret it. Likewise, if we're thinking of dream theories and interpretations or problems in our lives, we can't be fully listening to the dream and are in danger of forcing it into a framework we already have in mind. I once heard someone say that we don't need to kill the bird in order to study it; it's much better to let it sing— and the same is true with dreams.

A second aspect of listening to dreams is also made possible by writing them down—sooner or later we'll have collections of them we can review as a dream series. This series is like an ongoing conversation with our unconscious, the structure that supports our lives. One of my clients reviewed his dreams over a period of several months. He first read them over to get a feeling of their different emotional contents. Then he made a list of the main characters and their positive and negative attributes, a list of the places where the dreams took place, and a summary of their story lines and outcomes. He discovered that many of the dreams seemed to fit in the series like chapters in a larger story and his feelings in them appeared like nuances of color in a large painting. This activity can be fun as well as offering important insights into how we're growing and changing, and how some of our dearly held attitudes and beliefs are being consigned to the past.

Questioning

The questions we ask ourselves about our dreams can fall into as many areas as we can imagine. Just as examining a painting reveals its details and beauty, questioning a dream opens up the view of specific scenarios and leaves us wondering where is this place, who are these people, what are they like, why do they keep appearing? We may ask ourselves why this animal, this landscape, this concern or this dream is appearing in our lives at this particular moment. The unconscious is trying to tell us where our energy is, and where it's going in the plot or story line of the dream. With this in mind it becomes important to ask how the dream is developing and how it is concluding.

Reflecting

Reflecting on our dreams can be like selecting new clothes. We have to try them on, and if they seem to fit, we take them. Then we have to wear them for a while and move around in them until they feel comfortable. Similarly, we may mull over a dream's images and moods and consider the questions we've asked and the answers that come to mind as we're trying to figure out how the dream "fits." Finally, the dream's components may become part of our lives and change our habitual way of seeing things, especially ourselves. In other words, each little bit of new understanding we gain is something we integrate in a manner that expands our awareness.

AUTHOR'S BIO

Bud Harris, PhD, is a Jungian analyst, writer, and lecturer, who has dedicated his life to help people grow through their challenges and life situations to become "the best versions of themselves."

Originally a corporate businessman, Bud then owned his own business. Though very successful, he began to search for a new version of himself and his life at age thirty-five. He had become dissatisfied with his accomplishments in business and was being challenged by serious illness in his family.

Bud returned to graduate school to study psychotherapy. He earned his PhD in psychology and practiced as a psychotherapist and psychologist for several years. Later, Bud moved to Zurich, Switzerland, where he trained for over five years and graduated from the C. G. Jung Institute to become a Jungian analyst.

Bud is the author of over 20 informing and inspiring books. He writes and teaches with his wife, Jungian analyst Massimilla Harris, PhD, and lectures widely. Bud and Massimilla are practicing Jungian analysts in Asheville, North Carolina. For more information about Bud's practice and work, visit www.budharris.com and www.facebook.com/BudHarrisPh.D/.